The Vegan Chocolatier:
From Bean to Bliss

Stefan Kronas

Inhalt

Foreword

Dear Readers,

Welcome to a journey that will inspire your senses and ignite your creativity. In this book, we together open the door to the fascinating world of vegan chocolate-making—a universe filled with flavor, aroma, and pure joy.

These pages are more than just a collection of recipes; they are an invitation to explore, understand, and master the art of chocolate-making. Whether you are taking the first step towards a more sustainable lifestyle, rediscovering your passion for chocolate, or simply curious about how vegan chocolate is made— this book is for you.

I have designed this book with the intention of providing newcomers to the field with a comprehensive, easy-to-understand, and stimulating manual. From the basics to the fine details of chocolate production, including sustainable and ethical considerations, I aim to equip you with the tools to make your own vegan chocolate with confidence and joy.

However, this book is not just a one-way street of learning. We warmly invite you to become part of a community of chocolate lovers who wish to share, learn, and grow. Your experiences, successes, and even challenges on this journey are valuable—not just to you, but also to us and other readers.

Therefore, I encourage you, after reading this book and diving into the practice of chocolate-making, to leave a review. Share your thoughts, your progress, and of course, your delicious creations. Your feedback is not only a source of inspiration for others but also a guidepost for future editions of this book.

Consider this book as your faithful companion on the path to mastery in vegan chocolate-making. Let's discover, create, and enjoy together.

With sweet regards and looking forward to your creations,
Stefan Kronas

Introduction

Welcome to the fascinating world of vegan chocolate! This book is your ultimate guide through the artful and delicious landscape of plant-based sweets. Whether you are a passionate vegan, interested in sustainable eating, or just looking to expand your culinary horizons, making vegan chocolate offers endless opportunities to combine creativity and pleasure.

The Popularity of Vegan Chocolate
Vegan chocolate has evolved from a niche passion to a mainstream delight. Its growing popularity not only reflects the trend towards plant-based diets but also an increasing awareness of health, animal welfare, and environmental protection. Enjoying vegan chocolate means not just abstaining from animal products but also choosing a world where pleasure and ethical responsibility go hand in hand.

A Brief History of Chocolate
The history of chocolate is as rich and complex as its flavor. It began over 3,000 years ago with the cultures of the Maya and Aztecs, where the cocoa bean was not only valued as a precious ingredient for a cocoa-based drink but also used as currency. The Spanish conquerors brought cocoa to Europe, where it eventually became the beloved luxury item we know and love today. Over the centuries, chocolate has continuously evolved—from the bitter draught of ancient civilizations to the sweet, creamy indulgence on modern supermarket shelves.

The Journey to Veganism
Parallel to this, veganism has evolved from a philosophical conviction to a global movement that advocates for a life-affirming, ethically responsible way of living. Choosing vegan chocolate is an expression of this movement—it's about finding pleasure without compromising one's values.

What to Expect in This Book?
In the following chapters, we take you on a journey of discovery. From the basics of vegan chocolate making to creative recipes and sustainable practices—this book has everything you need to know to create your own vegan chocolate. We place special emphasis on making the information accessible and actionable,

so you can enjoy success regardless of your level of experience.

Prepare to dive into the delicious world of vegan chocolate. Be inspired, experiment with new ideas, and discover the joy of creating your own sweet masterpieces.

Your adventure starts now!

Fundamentals of Vegan Chocolate Making

Welcome to the second chapter of our adventure, where we explore the fundamentals of vegan chocolate making. Whether you already have experience in the kitchen or are just discovering your passion for creating chocolate, this chapter provides you with the necessary tools to begin your journey.

Ingredients: The Core of Vegan Chocolate
The creation of exquisite vegan chocolate starts with choosing the right ingredients. At the heart, of course, is the cocoa bean, whose quality and origin significantly influence the flavor of your chocolate. In addition to cocoa, there are other important ingredients that make your chocolate unique:

Cocoa Butter:
Provides the creamy texture and melt that we love in chocolate.

Sweeteners:
Whether it's cane sugar, coconut sugar, or maple syrup, choosing your sweetener can refine and vary the flavor of your chocolate.

Milk Alternatives:
For creating milk chocolate alternatives, almond milk powder, soy milk powder, or coconut milk powder, to name a few, give the chocolate a soft note and delicate texture.

Flavorings and Additives:
From vanilla to sea salt to nuts or dried fruits—these ingredients allow you to unleash your creativity and personalize your chocolate.

Equipment and Tools:

While the ingredients are the core, the right equipment is the foundation on which your chocolate creations are built. For starters, you'll need:

- Chocolate melter or double boiler: To gently melt the cocoa butter and chocolate.
- Chocolate molds: Available in various sizes and shapes, allowing you to customize your chocolate.
- Grinder or mortar: For finely grinding the cocoa beans and other ingredients.
- Thermometer: Precise temperature control is crucial for the texture and gloss of the finished chocolate.
- Spatula and whisk: For mixing and stirring the chocolate mixture.

First Steps in Chocolate Making

With the right ingredients and tools at your side, you are now ready to begin the process of chocolate making. Here is a simple guide to get you started:

Melting:

Begin by slowly melting the cocoa butter. Be sure to use a low temperature to preserve the fine flavors.

Mixing:

Once the cocoa butter is melted, add the cocoa mass (or cocoa powder) and your chosen sweetener. Stir well until a homogeneous mass is formed.

Refining:

Now is the moment to give your chocolate a personal touch by adding milk alternatives, flavorings, or additives.

Shaping:

Pour the chocolate mixture into the prepared molds. Gently tapping the molds on the work surface helps remove air bubbles.

Cooling:

Allow your chocolate to cool and set. It is best done at room temperature to avoid condensation.

With these basics, you are now well-equipped to dive into the world of vegan chocolate making. Each chapter that follows will deepen your skills and provide new techniques and inspirations.

Look forward to discovering
and enjoying your own
delicious creations!

Nutritional and Health Information on Vegan Chocolate

Vegan chocolate is more than just a treat for the senses; it also offers various health benefits that are often overlooked. Below, we will highlight the nutritional aspects and health benefits of plant-based ingredients in vegan chocolate.

- **Antioxidants in Cocoa:** Cocoa, the core ingredient in all chocolate, is rich in antioxidants, specifically flavonoids. These help the body fight free radicals, which can reduce inflammation and improve heart health.

- **Plant-based Milk Alternatives:** Instead of animal milk, our recipes use almond, soy, or coconut milk powder. These ingredients are not only suitable for those who are lactose intolerant or vegan but also provide valuable nutrients like vitamin E (in almond milk) or lauric acid (in coconut milk), which has antibacterial properties.

- **Natural Sweeteners:** Rather than refined sugar, we opt for natural sweeteners like coconut sugar or maple syrup. These not only add sweetness but also contain minerals and have a lower glycemic index, which can contribute to a more stable blood sugar level.

- **Nuts and Seeds:** Incorporating nuts and seeds into our chocolate recipes not only brings flavor diversity and texture but also essential fatty acids, proteins, and micronutrients such as magnesium and zinc.

These components make vegan chocolate a healthy choice, enriching your diet with nutrients that support overall well-being while satisfying your sweet tooth in a more wholesome way.

The Art of Chocolate Making

In the art of chocolate making, special considerations are required for creating the three main types of chocolate: dark, milk, and white vegan chocolate. Each type demands its own balance of ingredients and may require different temperatures and times for optimal results.

Dark Vegan Chocolate

The making of dark chocolate forms the foundation of chocolate art. Dark vegan chocolate is characterized by a high cocoa content, giving it a robust chocolate flavor.

Ingredient Ratio:
Approximately 70% cocoa mass, 15% cocoa butter, 15% sweetener.
Conching:
At about 80°C (176°F) for 2-6 hours, to achieve a smooth texture and the desired flavor balance.
Tempering:
Heat to 45°C (113°F), cool to 28°C (82°F), then reheat to 31-32°C (88-90°F).

Vegan Milk Chocolate

Vegan milk chocolate substitutes dairy with plant-based alternatives like almond, soy, or coconut milk powder, to achieve a creamy texture and a milder taste.

Ingredient Ratio:
45-55% cocoa mass, 10-20% cocoa butter, 5-10% plant-based milk powder, 20-30% sweetener.
Conching:
Since milk chocolate has a softer texture, conching can be slightly shorter, about 2-4 hours at 80°C (176°F).
Tempering: Heat to 45°C (113°F), cool to 28°C (82°F), then reheat to 29-30°C (84-86°F) for the ideal processing temperature.

White Vegan Chocolate

White chocolate contains no cocoa mass and is based on cocoa butter, sweeteners, and plant-based milk powders, giving it a delicate sweetness and creamy consistency.

Ingredient Ratio:
30-40% cocoa butter, 10-15% plant-based milk powder, 45-60% sweetener.
Conching:
Since white chocolate is more delicate, conching should occur at a slightly lower temperature, e.g., 75-78°C (167-172°F), for about 2-4 hours.
Tempering:
Heat to 40-42°C (104-108°F), cool to 26-27°C (79-81°F), then reheat to 28-29°C (82-84°F) to achieve the ideal consistency and shine.

With these specific instructions, you can now begin to master all three types of vegan chocolate. Each type of chocolate opens up its own universe of flavor profiles and textures. By experimenting with the proportions and processing, you may even discover your own unique chocolate creation.

Recipes for vegan chocolate

Basic Recipe - Vegan Dark Chocolate

Ingredients:

200g cocoa mass
100g cocoa butter
70-100g sweetener (to taste, e.g., coconut sugar)

Instructions:

Melting:
Melt the cocoa butter in a water bath at about 45°C (113°F). This ensures even melting without overheating.

Mixing:
At the same temperature (45°C), combine the melted cocoa butter with the cocoa mass and sweetener in a bowl until a homogeneous mass is formed. It is important to constantly stir the mixture to ensure even distribution of the ingredients.

Tempering:
Cool the chocolate mass to 28°C (82°F) and then reheat to 31-32°C (88-90°F). This step is crucial for the gloss and crisp texture of the finished chocolate.

Pouring:
Pour the tempered chocolate mass into molds. The chocolate should set at room temperature, which can take 1-2 hours depending on the room climate..

Basic Recipe - Vegan Milk Chocolate with Almond Milk Powder

Ingredients:

150g cocoa mass
100g cocoa butter
50g almond milk powder
100g sweetener (to taste)

Instructions:

Melting:
Carefully melt the cocoa butter in a water bath at about 45°C (113°F).

Mixing:
At the same temperature, add the cocoa mass, almond milk powder, and sweetener. Stir until the mixture is smooth.

Tempering:
Let the mixture cool to 28°C (82°F) and then warm it up to 29-30°C (84-86°F). This step helps achieve the ideal texture for vegan milk chocolate.

Pouring:
Fill the chocolate mass into molds and let it set, which typically takes 1-2 hours at room temperature.

These recipes provide a great foundation for creating delicious vegan chocolates, allowing you to enjoy the rich flavors and textures of traditional chocolate while adhering to vegan standards.

Basic Recipe - Vegan White Chocolate

Ingredients:

200g cocoa butter
60g coconut milk powder
140g powdered sugar (vegan)
Optional: Vanilla extract for additional flavor

Instructions:

Melting:
Melt the cocoa butter in a water bath at a low temperature (about 40-42°C or 104-108°F). It's especially important not to overheat white chocolate.

Mixing:
Add coconut milk powder and powdered sugar, stirring thoroughly. If desired, stir in vanilla extract.

Tempering:
Allow the mixture to cool to 26-27°C (79-81°F) and then reheat to 28-29°C (82-84°F). This promotes the shine and firmness of the white chocolate.

Pouring:
Pour the tempered chocolate into molds and let it set, which may take about 1-2 hours.

These precise instructions should help you make high-quality vegan chocolate with professional results. Tempering is a critical step that requires practice, but it's key to achieving chocolate with perfect gloss and a crisp bite. Experiment, have patience, and most importantly:

Enjoy the creative process of chocolate making!

Morning Wake-Up: Espresso & Walnut

Ingredients:

200g cocoa mass
100g cocoa butter
100g cane sugar (or another vegan sweetener of choice)
2 tbsp espresso, strong and cold
100g walnuts, roughly chopped
A pinch of sea salt

Preparation:

Roast the walnuts in a preheated oven at 180°C (356°F) for 8-10 minutes until they are lightly browned and aromatic. Let them cool and then chop them roughly.
Prepare a strong espresso and let it cool.

Melting the Cocoa Butter:

Place the cocoa butter in a heat-resistant vessel and melt it over a water bath on low heat. The ideal temperature for melting cocoa butter is about 40-45°C (104-113°F). Avoid overheating the cocoa butter to preserve its quality.

Adding the Cocoa Mass:

Once the cocoa butter is completely melted, add the cocoa mass. Stir continuously until the mixture is homogeneous and smooth.

Incorporating the Dry Ingredients:

Remove the vessel from the water bath and add the cane sugar. Stir well until the sugar has completely dissolved.
Now integrate the cooled espresso into the chocolate mixture. Ensure that the espresso is cold to avoid shocking the chocolate.

Tempering:

Cool the chocolate mass by stirring to about 28°C (82°F) and then reheat it to 31-32°C (88-90°F). This step is crucial for giving the chocolate a beautiful shine and a firm consistency.

Adding the Walnuts:

Once the chocolate is tempered, stir in the roasted walnut pieces and a pinch of sea salt. The walnuts not only add a crunchy bite but also a deep, nutty flavor that perfectly complements the espresso.

Pouring and Setting:

Pour the chocolate mixture into a prepared mold. Use a spatula to smooth the surface and ensure that the nuts are evenly distributed.
Allow the chocolate to set at room temperature. Depending on the room temperature, this can take 1-2 hours. For quicker setting, you can also place the chocolate in the refrigerator.

Serving:

Once the chocolate is completely set, you can release it from the mold and break or cut it into pieces.

Enjoy your homemade Morning Wake-Up chocolate as an invigorating start to the day or as a delicious afternoon snack.

This detailed guide helps you create an exquisite dark vegan chocolate with the invigorating taste of espresso and the crispy texture of walnuts. The process may seem elaborate at first glance, but the result is worth every effort – a perfectly balanced, handmade chocolate that will delight your palate.

Nutty Energizer - Hazelnut & Coffee

Ingredients:

150g cocoa mass
100g cocoa butter
50g almond milk powder (or other vegan milk powder)
80g coconut sugar (or other vegan sweetener)
2 tbsp instant coffee powder (or finely ground coffee for a more intense flavor)
100g hazelnuts, roasted and chopped
A pinch of salt

Preparing Hazelnuts:

Spread the hazelnuts on a baking sheet and roast at 180°C (356°F) for about 10-12 minutes until golden brown. After cooling, coarsely chop the hazelnuts.

Melting Cocoa Butter and Cocoa Mass:

Melt the cocoa butter in a water bath at a low temperature (about 40-45°C or 104-113°F). Once it's liquid, add the cocoa mass and stir constantly until a homogeneous mixture is formed.

Incorporating Dry Ingredients:

Add almond milk powder, coconut sugar, coffee powder, and a pinch of salt to the chocolate mixture. Stir well until all ingredients are fully integrated and the mixture is smooth.

Tempering the Chocolate:

To achieve a shiny surface and a crisp texture, cool the chocolate mixture to about 28°C (82°F) and then warm it to 29-30°C (84-86°F). This is particularly important for milk chocolate to reach the correct consistency.

Adding Hazelnuts:

Add the roasted hazelnut pieces to the tempered chocolate and stir well to evenly distribute them in the mixture.

Pouring and Setting:

Pour the finished chocolate mixture into prepared molds. Use a spatula to smooth the surface.
Allow the chocolate to set at room temperature, which can take 1-2 hours depending on the temperature. A cool, dry place is ideal.

Enjoy:

Once set, release the chocolate from the molds and break or cut it into desired pieces.

The Nutty Energizer is now ready to enjoy. The combination of hazelnut and coffee makes this vegan milk chocolate a perfect companion for any coffee break.

This recipe combines the creamy texture of vegan milk chocolate with the aromatic richness of coffee and the nutty notes of hazelnuts into an irresistible taste experience. Every bite of the Nutty Energizer awakens the senses and offers a luxurious treat that will delight both chocolate lovers and coffee aficionados.

Green Temptation - Matcha & Raspberry

Ingredients:

200g cocoa butter
50g coconut milk powder (or other vegan milk powder)
120g powdered sugar (vegan)
2 tsp high-quality matcha powder
100g raspberries (fresh or freeze-dried)
A pinch of salt

Preparing the Raspberries:

If using fresh raspberries, place them on a baking sheet and freeze until hard. Skip this step for freeze-dried raspberries.

Melting Cocoa Butter:

Break the cocoa butter into small pieces and gently melt it over a water bath on low heat. The ideal temperature for melting cocoa butter is about 40-42°C (104-108°F).

Incorporating Dry Ingredients:

Once the cocoa butter is melted, remove the vessel from the water bath. Sift in the powdered sugar and coconut milk powder to avoid lumps, and stir the mixture until smooth.
Add the matcha powder and stir thoroughly to achieve an even green color. Add a pinch of salt to enhance the flavor notes.

Tempering the Chocolate:

Cool the chocolate mixture by stirring to about 26-27°C (79-81°F) and then warm it again to 28-29°C (82-84°F). Tempering is crucial for the texture and shine of the white chocolate.

Adding the Raspberries:

Lightly crush the frozen or freeze-dried raspberries into smaller pieces. Carefully fold them into the tempered chocolate mixture to ensure even distribution. Avoid stirring too much to prevent the raspberries from breaking down too much and turning the mixture pink.

Pouring and Setting:

Pour the chocolate mixture into chocolate molds. Use a spatula to evenly distribute the mixture and create a smooth surface.
Allow the chocolate to set at room temperature, which can take between 1-2 hours depending on the ambient temperature.

Enjoy:

Once the chocolate has set, release it from the molds and break or cut into pieces.

Green Temptation is ready to enjoy. The combination of matcha's bittersweet note and the fruity freshness of raspberries makes this white vegan chocolate a unique taste experience.

This recipe offers an exquisite blend of the rich flavors of matcha and the sweetness of raspberries, nestled in the creamy delicacy of white chocolate. Green Temptation is not just a visual treat but also a feast for the palate, showcasing the diversity of vegan chocolate creations.

Salty Sweetness - Sea Salt & Caramel

Ingredients for Vegan Caramel:

200ml coconut milk
100g coconut sugar
A pinch of salt
1 tsp vanilla extract (optional for additional flavor)

Ingredients for Chocolate:

200g cocoa mass
100g cocoa butter
100g coconut sugar
50g vegan caramel (made from coconut milk and coconut sugar)
Coarse sea salt for sprinkling

Preparation of Vegan Caramel:

Prepare the Caramel: In a medium saucepan, bring coconut milk, coconut sugar, and a pinch of salt to a boil over medium heat. Stir until the sugar has completely dissolved.
Thicken: Reduce the heat and simmer the mixture, stirring occasionally, for about 20-25 minutes until it thickens. Remove from heat and stir in vanilla extract. Let cool.

Making the Chocolate:

Melting:
Melt the cocoa butter in a water bath at low temperature (about 40-45°C or 104-113°F). Once liquid, add the cocoa mass and stir constantly until melted.

Sweetening:
Remove the chocolate mixture from the water bath and stir in coconut sugar (and optionally, vanilla extract) until smooth.

Tempering:
Cool the chocolate mass to about 28°C (82°F) and then warm it back up

to 31-32°C (88-90°F). This step is crucial for the shine and crisp texture of the finished chocolate.

Layering:
Pour a third of the chocolate mixture into a prepared mold. Distribute several teaspoons of the cooled caramel over it. Repeat this process until all ingredients are used up, ending with a layer of chocolate.

Sprinkling Sea Salt:
Immediately after pouring the last layer of chocolate, sprinkle coarse sea salt over the surface. The amount of salt can be adjusted to taste.

Setting:
Let the chocolate set at room temperature, which can take 1-2 hours depending on the room climate. For faster setting, the chocolate can also be placed in the refrigerator.

Serving:
Once set, release the chocolate from the mold and break or cut it into pieces. Salty Sweetness is now ready to enjoy.

This creation combines the deep intensity of dark chocolate with the creamy sweetness of vegan caramel, finished with a crispy, salty edge from the sea salt. Each bite offers a balanced taste experience that challenges and delights the senses. Salty Sweetness pays homage to the complexity and layers of flavors in vegan chocolate making, providing a luxurious treat that's both indulgent and sophisticated.

Tropical Crunch Time - Banana Chips & Walnut

Ingredients:

150g cocoa mass
100g cocoa butter
50g soy milk powder (or other vegan milk powder)
100g cane sugar
1 tsp vanilla extract
50g banana chips, lightly crushed
50g walnuts, roasted and chopped
A pinch of salt

Preparing the Ingredients:

Roast the walnuts at 180°C (356°F) for about 8-10 minutes until they are aromatic. After cooling, coarsely chop them.
Break the banana chips into smaller pieces, but not too fine, to maintain a crunchy texture.

Melting Cocoa Butter and Cocoa Mass:

Melt the cocoa butter in a water bath at a temperature of about 40-45°C (104-113°F). Once liquid, add the cocoa mass and stir until melted and smooth.

Incorporating Ingredients:

Remove the mixture from the water bath and stir in soy milk powder, cane sugar, vanilla extract, and a pinch of salt until well mixed and completely dissolved.

Tempering the Chocolate:

Cool the chocolate mixture to about 28°C (82°F) and then warm it back up to 29-30°C (84-86°F) to achieve the ideal texture and shine of milk chocolate.

Adding Banana Chips and Walnuts:

Fold the crushed banana chips and chopped walnuts into the tempered chocolate mixture, ensuring they are evenly distributed.

Pouring and Setting:

Pour the finished chocolate mixture into prepared molds. Use a spatula to evenly smooth the surface and ensure that the banana chips and walnuts are well embedded.
Allow the chocolate to set at room temperature, which can take 1-2 hours depending on the ambient temperature.

Serving:

Once the chocolate is set, release it from the molds and break or cut into pieces.

Tropical Crunch Time offers a delightful combination of creamy vegan milk chocolate texture, sweet crunch from the banana chips, and nutty flavor from the walnuts. A perfect snack for any time of the day.

This chocolate creation brings a slice of the tropics into your kitchen, combining the delightful flavors of banana and walnut with the gentle sweetness of vegan milk chocolate. An exquisite choice for those looking for a sweet escape with a crunchy surprise.

Lemon Poppyseed Magic - Lemon & Poppy

Ingredients:

200g cocoa butter
60g almond milk powder (or other vegan milk powder)
120g powdered sugar (vegan)
Zest of 2 organic lemons
2 tbsp lemon juice
3 tbsp poppy seeds
A pinch of salt

Preparation:

Thoroughly wash the lemons and zest them, making sure to use only the yellow layer, as the white is bitter.
Squeeze the juice from the lemons and set it aside.

Melting Cocoa Butter:

Break the cocoa butter into smaller pieces and melt it in a water bath at a low temperature (about 40-42°C or 104-108°F). Ensure that water does not get into the chocolate.

Incorporating Dry Ingredients:

Once the cocoa butter is melted, remove it from the water bath and sift in the powdered sugar and almond milk powder to avoid lumps. Stir the mixture until smooth.

Adding Flavors:

Add the lemon zest, lemon juice, and poppy seeds. Stir well to distribute all the flavors evenly. Add a pinch of salt to enhance the flavor notes.

Tempering the Chocolate:

Cool the chocolate mixture by stirring to about 26-27°C (79-81°F) and then warm it again to 28-29°C (82-84°F). Tempering is crucial for the texture and shine of the white chocolate.

Pouring and Setting:

Pour the chocolate mixture into prepared molds. Use a spatula to evenly distribute the mixture and create a smooth surface.
Allow the chocolate to set at room temperature, which can take 1-2 hours depending on the ambient temperature.

Enjoy:

Once the chocolate is set, release it from the molds and break or cut into pieces.

Lemon Poppyseed Magic is ready to enjoy. This creation combines the creaminess of white chocolate with the refreshing aroma of lemon and the crispy contrast of poppy seeds for an unforgettable taste experience.

This chocolate creation offers a wonderful balance of sweetness and acidity with a hint of crispiness, ideal for those seeking an exceptional flavor combination. Lemon Poppyseed Magic is an excellent choice for special occasions or as a refreshing treat on a warm day.

Fiery Citrus Night - Orange & Ginger

Ingredients:

200g cocoa mass
100g cocoa butter
100g fine cane sugar
Zest of 1 organic orange
2 tbsp freshly squeezed orange juice
2 tbsp fresh ginger, finely grated
A pinch of hot chili powder (optional, depending on desired spiciness)
A pinch of salt

Preparation:

Thoroughly wash the orange and zest it. Be careful to use only the colored part of the peel to avoid bitterness.
Squeeze the juice from the orange and set it aside.
Peel and finely grate the ginger.

Melting Cocoa Butter and Cocoa Mass:

Break the cocoa butter and cocoa mass into smaller pieces and melt them in a water bath at low temperature (about 40-45°C or 104-113°F). Stir continuously to ensure an even melt.

Stirring in Sugar and Flavors:

Remove the chocolate mixture from the water bath and stir in the cane sugar until fully dissolved.
Add the orange zest, orange juice, and freshly grated ginger. If you like a spicy kick, add a pinch of chili powder now. Stir well.

Tempering the Chocolate:

Cool the chocolate mixture by stirring to about 28°C (82°F) and then warm it back up to 31-32°C (88-90°F). Tempering ensures a shine and crisp texture.

Pouring and Setting:

Pour the tempered chocolate mixture into prepared chocolate molds. Use a spatula to achieve a smooth surface.
Allow the chocolate to set at room temperature, which can take 1-2 hours depending on the room climate.

Serving:

Once the chocolate is set, carefully release it from the molds and break or cut into pieces.

Fiery Citrus Night is ready to enjoy. This vegan dark chocolate combines the sweetness of orange with the sharpness of ginger and the optional heat of chili for an exciting taste experience.

This creative chocolate creation plays with the contrast of sweet and spicy, offering a unique sensory experience. Fiery Citrus Night is perfect as a special treat for bold gourmets or as a highlight of any chocolate lover's gathering.

Sweet Gold - Date Caramel & Fleur de Sel

Ingredients for Date Caramel:

200g Medjool dates, pitted and chopped
100ml coconut milk
1 tsp vanilla extract
A pinch of salt

Ingredients for Chocolate:

150g cocoa mass
100g cocoa butter
50g almond milk powder (or other vegan milk powder)
100g fine cane sugar
Fleur de Sel for sprinkling

Date Caramel Preparation:

In a blender, process the chopped dates, coconut milk, vanilla extract, and a pinch of salt into a smooth paste.
Heat the mixture in a saucepan over low heat until it slightly thickens, stirring regularly to prevent burning. Let it cool down afterwards.

Melting Cocoa Butter and Cocoa Mass:

Break the cocoa butter and cocoa mass into small pieces and melt them over a water bath at a temperature of about 40-45°C (104-113°F), stirring constantly for an even melt.

Stirring in Milk Powder and Sugar:

Remove the chocolate mixture from the water bath and stir in the almond milk powder and cane sugar until well mixed and the sugar is completely dissolved.

Tempering the Chocolate:

To achieve a shiny surface and firm texture, cool the chocolate mixture by stirring to about 28°C (82°F) and then warm it back up to 29-30°C (84-86°F).

Pouring the Chocolate:

Pour a thin layer of the chocolate mixture into prepared chocolate molds and let it set briefly. Then add a teaspoon of the date caramel on top of the chocolate layer and cover it with more chocolate until the mold is filled.

Sprinkling with Fleur de Sel:

Immediately after filling the molds, sprinkle a light dusting of Fleur de Sel over the chocolate.

Setting:

Allow the chocolate to set at room temperature, which can take 1-2 hours depending on the room climate.

Serving:

Once the chocolate is set, release it from the molds and break or cut into pieces.

Sweet Gold combines the natural sweetness of date caramel with the gentle note of vegan milk chocolate and a touch of Fleur de Sel for a balanced sweet-salty indulgence.

Sweet Gold is an exquisite fusion of flavors that delights the palate with the sweetness of dates, the creaminess of vegan milk chocolate, and the crackling contrast of Fleur de Sel. A luxurious creation that gilds the moment.

Strawberry Basil Marvel - Strawberry & Basil

Ingredients:

200g cocoa butter
60g cashew milk powder (or other vegan milk powder)
120g powdered sugar (vegan)
100g strawberries, fresh or freeze-dried, finely chopped
2 tbsp fresh basil, finely chopped
A pinch of salt

Preparation:

If using fresh strawberries, wash, remove the stems, and finely chop. For a more intense color and flavor, the strawberries can be marinated with a bit of sugar and left in the refrigerator for a few hours before use. If using freeze-dried strawberries, finely chop them directly.
Wash, dry, and finely chop the basil.

Melting Cocoa Butter:

Break the cocoa butter into small pieces and melt it over a water bath at a temperature of about 40-42°C (104-108°F), stirring constantly for an even melt.

Incorporating Dry Ingredients:

Once the cocoa butter is melted, remove the vessel from the water bath. Sift in the powdered sugar and cashew milk powder and stir until the mixture is smooth.

Adding Flavors:

Add the chopped strawberries and chopped basil to the chocolate mixture. Stir gently to ensure even distribution. Add a pinch of salt to balance the flavor notes.

Tempering the Chocolate:

To achieve an optimal texture and shine, cool the chocolate mixture by stirring to about 26-27°C (79-81°F) and then warm it back up to 28-29°C (82-84°F).

Pouring and Setting:

Pour the chocolate mixture into prepared chocolate molds. Use a spatula to ensure even distribution.
Allow the chocolate to set at room temperature, which can take 1-2 hours depending on the room climate.
Serving:

Once the chocolate is set, release it from the molds and break or cut into pieces.

Strawberry Basil Marvel combines the sweetness of strawberries with the fresh note of basil in a delicate vegan white chocolate. A creation that brings the essence of summer to your taste buds.

Strawberry Basil Marvel is a refreshing and aromatic combination that captures the lightness of summer. This vegan white chocolate is perfect for anyone looking for a sweet indulgence with a herbal note. A true marvel of flavors that delights on any occasion.

Spicy Citrus Kick - Chili & Lime

Ingredients:

200g cocoa mass
100g cocoa butter
100g cane sugar
Zest of 2 organic limes
2 tbsp freshly squeezed lime juice
1 tsp finely ground chili (adjust to taste)
A pinch of salt

Preparation:

Thoroughly wash the limes and finely zest them, ensuring to use only the green layer to avoid bitterness.
Squeeze the juice from the limes and set it aside.

Melting Cocoa Butter and Cocoa Mass:

Brechen Sie die Kakaobutter und Kakaomasse in kleinere Stücke und schmelzen Sie diese in einem Wasserbad bei niedriger Temperatur (ca. 40-45°C). Stetiges Rühren gewährleistet eine gleichmäßige Schmelze.

Stirring in Sugar, Flavors, and Spices:

Remove the chocolate mixture from the water bath and stir in the cane sugar until fully dissolved.
Add the lime zest, lime juice, and ground chili. Add a pinch of salt to enhance the flavor notes. Stir well to achieve a homogeneous distribution.

Tempering the Chocolate:

Cool the chocolate mixture by stirring to about 28°C (82°F) and then warm it back up to 31-32°C (88-90°F). This tempering ensures a beautiful shine and crisp consistency of the chocolate.

Pouring and Setting:

Pour the tempered chocolate mixture into prepared chocolate molds. Use a spatula to ensure even distribution.
Allow the chocolate to set at room temperature, which can take 1-2 hours depending on the room climate.

Serving:

Once the chocolate is set, release it from the molds and break or cut into pieces.

Spicy Citrus Kick offers an exciting flavor combination of lime's acidity and chili's heat, embedded in the depth of dark chocolate. A creation for those seeking a taste explosion.

This vegan dark chocolate creation blends the refreshing taste of lime with the pleasant heat of chili. Spicy Citrus Kick is perfect for those who love to challenge their taste buds and discover new, daring combinations. An irresistible treat that masterfully maintains the balance between sweetness, acidity, and spiciness.

Lavender Dream - Apricot & Lavender

Ingredients:

150g cocoa mass
100g cocoa butter
50g rice milk powder (or other vegan milk powder)
100g fine cane sugar
2 tsp dried culinary lavender flowers
100g dried apricots, finely chopped
A pinch of salt

Preparing the Ingredients:

Cut the dried apricots into small pieces to ensure an even distribution in the chocolate. The pieces should not be too large.
Have the lavender flowers ready, ensuring to use culinary lavender suitable for consumption.

Melting Cocoa Butter and Cocoa Mass:

Break the cocoa butter and cocoa mass into smaller pieces and melt them in a water bath at a temperature of about 40-45°C (104-113°F), stirring constantly for an even melt.

Stirring in Milk Powder and Sugar:

Remove the chocolate mixture from the water bath and stir in the rice milk powder and cane sugar until well mixed and the sugar is completely dissolved.

Adding Lavender and Apricots:

Add the lavender flowers and chopped apricots to the chocolate mixture. Stir well to ensure the ingredients are evenly distributed.

Tempering the Chocolate:

To achieve a shiny surface and crisp texture, cool the chocolate mixture by stirring to about 28°C (82°F) and then warm it back up to 29-30°C (84-86°F).

Pouring and Setting:

Pour the tempered chocolate mixture into chocolate molds. Use a spatula to evenly distribute the mixture in the molds.
Allow the chocolate to set at room temperature, which can take 1-2 hours depending on the ambient temperature.

Serving:

Once the chocolate is set, release it from the molds and cut or break into pieces.

Lavender Dream combines the delicate sweetness of apricots with the aromatic depth of lavender in a creamy vegan milk chocolate. A taste experience that invites you to dream.

This chocolate creation is a tribute to the gentle flavors of spring and summer. The combination of lavender and apricot in the creamy base of vegan milk chocolate creates an incomparable taste experience that is both refreshing and soothing. Lavender Dream is perfect for moments when you want to indulge in a sweet escape.

Exotic Crunch - Passion Fruit & Crunchy Quinoa

Ingredients:

200g cocoa butter
60g coconut milk powder (or other vegan milk powder)
120g powdered sugar (vegan)
100g passion fruit pulp (from fresh passion fruits or pre-made pulp)
50g quinoa, puffed and lightly toasted for extra crunch
A pinch of salt

Preparation:

If using fresh passion fruits, halve them and scoop out the flesh. Press the flesh through a sieve to remove the seeds and obtain the pulp.
Toast the quinoa in a dry pan over medium heat until it's lightly puffed and golden. Let it cool completely.

Melting Cocoa Butter:

Break the cocoa butter into small pieces and melt it over a water bath at a temperature of about 40-42°C (104-108°F), stirring constantly for an even melt.

Incorporating Dry Ingredients:

Once the cocoa butter is melted, remove the vessel from the water bath. Sift in the powdered sugar and coconut milk powder and stir until the mixture is smooth.

Adding Flavors:

Add the passion fruit pulp to the chocolate mixture and stir thoroughly to evenly distribute the flavors. Add a pinch of salt to balance the flavor notes.

Stirring in Quinoa:

Fold the toasted, puffed quinoa into the chocolate mixture, stirring gently to ensure even distribution while preserving the crunch.

Tempering the Chocolate:

To achieve an optimal texture and shine, cool the chocolate mixture by stirring to about 26-27°C (79-81°F) and then warm it back up to 28-29°C (82-84°F).

Pouring and Setting:

Pour the chocolate mixture into prepared chocolate molds. Use a spatula to ensure even distribution.
Allow the chocolate to set at room temperature, which can take 1-2 hours depending on the ambient temperature.

Serving:

Once the chocolate is set, release it from the molds and break or cut into pieces.

Exotic Crunch is a unique combination of tropical tartness from passion fruit and pleasant crunch from quinoa, embedded in creamy white chocolate. A creation that invites you on a flavorful journey of discovery.

Exotic Crunch combines exotic flavors with a surprising texture for an irresistible taste experience. This vegan white chocolate is an ode to creativity and diversity in vegan cuisine, perfect for those seeking new and inspiring flavors.

Fresh Cocoa Explosion - Mint & Cocoa Nibs

Ingredients:

200g cocoa mass
100g cocoa butter
100g fine cane sugar
2-3 tbsp fresh mint, finely chopped
50g cacao nibs
A pinch of salt

Preparation:

Thoroughly wash, dry, and finely chop the fresh mint to optimally release its aroma.
Have the cacao nibs ready. For additional roasted notes, lightly toast the cacao nibs in a dry pan over low heat for a few minutes. Let them cool afterwards.

Melting Cocoa Butter and Cocoa Mass:

Break the cocoa butter and cocoa mass into smaller pieces and melt them over a water bath at a temperature of about 40-45°C (104-113°F), stirring constantly for an even melt.

Stirring in Sugar:

Remove the chocolate mixture from the water bath and stir in the cane sugar until well mixed and the sugar is completely dissolved.

Adding Mint:

Add the chopped mint to the chocolate mixture and stir thoroughly to evenly distribute the flavors.

Tempering the Chocolate:

To achieve a shiny surface and firm texture, cool the chocolate mixture by stirring to about 28°C (82°F) and then warm it back up to 31-32°C (88-90°F).

Incorporating Cacao Nibs:

Sprinkle the cacao nibs over the still liquid chocolate in the molds after filling them about halfway. Then add the remaining chocolate mixture to encase the nibs.

Pouring and Setting:

Complete filling the chocolate molds and use a spatula to ensure even distribution.
Allow the chocolate to set at room temperature, which can take 1-2 hours depending on the ambient temperature.

Serving:

Once the chocolate is set, release it from the molds and break or cut into pieces.

Fresh Cocoa Explosion offers a refreshing flavor combination of the freshness of mint and the crunchy texture of cacao nibs, enveloped in rich dark chocolate. A perfect balance between sweetness and intense cocoa flavor.

Fresh Cocoa Explosion is a dark chocolate creation that combines the classic flavor of mint with the raw, unadulterated power of cacao nibs. This recipe pays homage to the deep and complex world of cocoa, offering an intense taste experience that revitalizes and refreshes the senses.

Tropical Paradise - Mango & Coconut

Ingredients:

150g cocoa mass
100g cocoa butter
50g coconut milk powder (or other vegan milk powder)
100g fine cane sugar
100g freeze-dried mango, finely chopped
50g unsweetened coconut flakes
A pinch of salt

Preparing the Ingredients:

Chop the freeze-dried mango into small, bite-sized pieces. Have the coconut flakes ready.

Melting Cocoa Butter and Cocoa Mass:

Break the cocoa butter and cocoa mass into smaller pieces and melt them over a water bath at a temperature of about 40-45°C (104-113°F), stirring constantly.

Stirring in Milk Powder and Sugar:

Remove the mixture from the water bath and stir in the coconut milk powder and cane sugar until fully integrated and the sugar is dissolved.

Adding Mango and Coconut Flakes:

Add the chopped mango and coconut flakes to the chocolate mixture. Stir gently to ensure even distribution without breaking down the mango too much.

Tempering the Chocolate:

Cool the chocolate mixture to about 28°C (82°F) and then warm it back up to 29-30°C (84-86°F). This step helps achieve a shiny surface and good consistency of the chocolate.

Pouring and Setting:

Pour the chocolate mixture into prepared molds. Use a spatula to smooth the surface and distribute the ingredients evenly.
Allow the chocolate to set at room temperature, which can take 1-2 hours depending on the ambient temperature.

Serving:

Once the chocolate is set, release it from the molds and break or cut into pieces.

Tropical Paradise transports you to a world of exotic flavors with every bite, combining the sweetness of mango with the creamy texture of vegan milk chocolate and the crispy contrast of coconut flakes.

This creation blends the exotic flavors of mango and coconut in a harmonious mix, enveloped by the creamy smoothness of vegan milk chocolate. Tropical Paradise is perfect for those seeking a touch of exoticism in their chocolate indulgence.

Lemon Lavender Harmony - Lemon & Lavender

Ingredients:

200g cocoa butter
60g almond milk powder (or other vegan milk powder)
120g powdered sugar (vegan)
Zest of 1 organic lemon
2 tbsp freshly squeezed lemon juice
1 tsp dried culinary lavender flowers
A pinch of salt

Preparation:

Thoroughly wash the lemon and zest it to obtain the lemon zest. Be careful to use only the outer, colored part of the peel to avoid bitterness. Squeeze the lemon to obtain the juice.

Melting Cocoa Butter:

Break the cocoa butter into small pieces and melt it over a water bath at a temperature of about 40-42°C (104-108°F). Ensure the water does not boil to prevent overheating.

Incorporating Dry Ingredients:

Once the cocoa butter is completely melted, remove the vessel from the water bath. Sift in the powdered sugar and almond milk powder and stir the mixture until completely smooth.

Adding Flavors:

Add the lemon zest, lemon juice, and lavender flowers. Stir until all ingredients are well distributed. Add a pinch of salt to balance the flavor notes.

Tempering the Chocolate:

To achieve an optimal texture and shine, cool the chocolate mixture by stirring to about 26-27°C (79-81°F) and then warm it back up to 28-29°C (82-84°F).

Pouring and Setting:

Pour the chocolate mixture into prepared molds. Use a spatula to smooth the surface and ensure the mixture is evenly distributed.
Allow the chocolate to set at room temperature, which can take 1-2 hours depending on the ambient temperature.

Serving:

Once the chocolate is set, release it from the molds and break or cut into pieces.

Lemon Lavender Harmony combines the freshness of lemon with the floral note of lavender in a velvety white chocolate.

This creation is an expression of elegance and refinement, perfect for those seeking an exceptional flavor combination. The exquisite blend of lemon and lavender in white chocolate offers a unique taste experience that is both invigorating and soothing. Lemon Lavender Harmony is excellent as a special gift or as a fine delicacy for special occasions.

Rosy Raspberry Love - Raspberry & Rose

Ingredients:

200g cocoa mass
100g cocoa butter
100g fine cane sugar
100g freeze-dried raspberries, lightly crushed
2 tsp rose water
Edible rose petals (optional, for decoration)
A pinch of salt

Preparing the Ingredients:

Prepare the freeze-dried raspberries by lightly crushing them to create smaller pieces and enhance the flavor.
If using, prepare the edible rose petals by carefully washing and drying them.

Melting Cocoa Butter and Cocoa Mass:

Break the cocoa butter and cocoa mass into smaller pieces and melt them over a water bath at a temperature of about 40-45°C (104-113°F), stirring constantly to ensure an even melt.

Stirring in Sugar:

Remove the chocolate mixture from the water bath and stir in the cane sugar until well mixed and the sugar is completely dissolved.

Adding Rose Water:

Add the rose water to the chocolate mixture and stir thoroughly to evenly distribute the flavors.

Tempering the Chocolate:

To achieve a shiny surface and firm texture, cool the chocolate mixture by stirring to about 28°C (82°F) and then warm it back up to 31-32°C (88-90°F).

Incorporating Raspberries:

Sprinkle the crushed raspberries over the still liquid chocolate in the molds after filling them about halfway. Then add the remaining chocolate mixture to encase the raspberries. For an extra decorative touch, place some edible rose petals on top of the chocolate before it sets completely.

Pouring and Setting:

Complete filling the chocolate molds and use a spatula to ensure even distribution.
Allow the chocolate to set at room temperature, which can take 1-2 hours depending on the ambient temperature.

Serving:

Once the chocolate is set, release it from the molds and break or cut into pieces.

Rosy Raspberry Love combines the delicate sweetness of raspberries with the subtle fragrance of roses in a luxurious dark chocolate. This creation is a declaration of love to the elegant harmony of natural flavors.

Rosy Raspberry Love is a dark chocolate creation that merges the fruity freshness of raspberries with the floral elegance of roses. The perfect balance of these flavors makes each chocolate bar a unique sensory experience that invites dreaming and enjoyment. This chocolate is ideal for those who appreciate the sophisticated interplay of fruit and floral notes in their treats.

Summer Garden - Strawberry & Basil

Ingredients:

150g cocoa mass
100g cocoa butter
50g oat milk powder (or other vegan milk powder)
100g fine cane sugar
100g strawberries, fresh or freeze-dried, finely chopped
2 tbsp basil, fresh and finely chopped
A pinch of salt

Preparing the Ingredients:

If using fresh strawberries, wash and thoroughly dry them, then finely chop. If using freeze-dried strawberries, chop them directly.
Wash the basil, dry it, and finely chop the leaves.

Melting Cocoa Butter and Cocoa Mass:

Break the cocoa butter and cocoa mass into small pieces and melt them in a water bath at about 40-45°C (104-113°F), stirring constantly to ensure an even melt.

Stirring in Milk Powder and Sugar:

Remove the chocolate mixture from the water bath and stir in the oat milk powder and cane sugar until well mixed and the sugar is completely dissolved.

Adding Strawberries and Basil:

Add the chopped strawberries and basil to the chocolate mixture. Stir gently to ensure even distribution.

Tempering the Chocolate:

To achieve an optimal texture and shine, cool the chocolate mixture by stirring to about 28°C (82°F) and then warm it back up to 29-30°C (84-86°F).

Pouring and Setting:

Pour the chocolate mixture into prepared molds. Use a spatula to ensure even distribution.
Allow the chocolate to set at room temperature, which can take 1-2 hours depending on the ambient temperature.

Serving:

Once the chocolate is set, release it from the molds and break or cut into pieces.

Summer Garden is a tribute to the light and fresh flavors of summer, combined in a creamy vegan milk chocolate. The sweet fruitiness of the strawberries perfectly complements the aromatic freshness of the basil.

This vegan milk chocolate offers a taste experience reminiscent of warm summer days in the garden. Summer Garden is excellent as an afternoon treat or a special sweet delight that is sure to impress friends and family.

Rose Garden Feast - Rose & Pistachio

Ingredients:

200g cocoa butter
60g almond milk powder (or other vegan milk powder)
120g powdered sugar (vegan)
2 tbsp rose water
1 tsp edible dried rose petals
50g pistachios, unsalted and chopped
A pinch of salt

Preparing the Ingredients:

Prepare the pistachios by coarsely chopping them. Ensure to use unsalted pistachios to control the flavor.
Have the edible rose petals ready, ensuring they are intended for culinary use.

Melting Cocoa Butter:

Break the cocoa butter into small pieces and melt it over a water bath at a temperature of about 40-42°C (104-108°F). Ensure the water does not boil to prevent overheating.

Incorporating Dry Ingredients and Flavors:

Once the cocoa butter is melted, remove the vessel from the water bath. Sift in the powdered sugar and almond milk powder and stir until the mixture is smooth.
Add the rose water and stir thoroughly to evenly distribute the flavors.

Adding Pistachios and Rose Petals:

Add the chopped pistachios and edible rose petals to the chocolate mixture. Stir gently to ensure even distribution without crushing the ingredients.

Tempering the Chocolate:

To achieve a shiny surface and firm texture, cool the chocolate mixture by stirring to about 26-27°C (79-81°F) and then warm it back up to 28-29°C (82-84°F).

Pouring and Setting:

Pour the chocolate mixture into prepared chocolate molds. Use a spatula to ensure even distribution.
Allow the chocolate to set at room temperature, which can take 1-2 hours depending on the ambient temperature.

Serving:

Once the chocolate is set, release it from the molds and break or cut into pieces.

Rose Garden Feast captivates with the delicate aroma of rose water, the visual appeal of rose petals, and the crunchy bite of pistachios. This vegan white chocolate is a true celebration of the senses.

Rose Garden Feast brings the elegance and fragrance of a blooming rose garden into the form of white chocolate. The combination of roses and pistachios creates a memorable taste experience, ideal for special occasions or as a sophisticated gift.

Lavender Berry Magic - Lavender & Blueberry

Ingredients:

200g cocoa mass
100g cocoa butter
100g fine cane sugar
2 tsp dried culinary lavender flowers
100g fresh blueberries (or freeze-dried blueberries)
A pinch of salt

Preparing the Ingredients:

If using fresh blueberries, wash them carefully and dry them completely. If using freeze-dried blueberries, this step is not necessary.
Prepare the lavender flowers, ensuring they are specifically intended for culinary use.

Melting Cocoa Butter and Cocoa Mass:

Break the cocoa butter and cocoa mass into small pieces and melt them over a water bath at about 40-45°C (104-113°F), stirring constantly to ensure an even melt.

Stirring in Sugar and Lavender:

Remove the chocolate mixture from the water bath and stir in the cane sugar and lavender flowers until well mixed and the sugar is completely dissolved.

Tempering the Chocolate:

To achieve an optimal consistency and shine, cool the chocolate mixture by stirring to about 28°C (82°F) and then warm it back up to 31-32°C (88-90°F).

Adding Blueberries:

Gently fold the blueberries into the tempered chocolate mixture, stirring gently to ensure even distribution and to avoid crushing the berries.

Pouring and Setting:

Pour the finished chocolate mixture into prepared chocolate molds. Use a spatula to ensure even distribution.
Allow the chocolate to set at room temperature, which can take 1-2 hours depending on the ambient temperature.

Serving:

Once the chocolate is set, release it from the molds and break or cut into pieces.

Lavender Berry Magic combines the floral taste of lavender with the natural sweetness of blueberries in a rich dark chocolate. This creation offers a unique taste experience that is both soothing and invigorating.

This dark vegan chocolate with lavender and blueberry is an exquisite blend ideal for both enjoyment and gifting. The gentle note of lavender perfectly complements the sweetness of the blueberries, embedded in the depth and richness of dark chocolate. Lavender Berry Magic demonstrates the diversity and endless possibilities in the world of vegan chocolate creations.

Vanilla Cashew Bliss - Vanilla & Cashew

Ingredients:

150g cocoa mass
100g cocoa butter
50g soy milk powder (or other vegan milk powder)
100g fine cane sugar
2 tsp vanilla extract (or seeds from one vanilla pod)
100g cashews, roasted and coarsely chopped
A pinch of salt

Preparing the Ingredients:

Spread the cashews on a baking sheet and roast at 180°C (356°F) for about 10 minutes until golden brown and fragrant. After cooling, coarsely chop them.

Melting Cocoa Butter and Cocoa Mass:

Break the cocoa butter and cocoa mass into smaller pieces and melt them in a water bath at about 40-45°C (104-113°F), stirring constantly to ensure an even melt.

Incorporating Milk Powder, Sugar, and Vanilla:

Remove the chocolate mixture from the water bath and stir in the soy milk powder, cane sugar, and vanilla extract until well mixed and the sugar is completely dissolved.

Adding Cashews:

Add the chopped cashews to the chocolate mixture and stir gently to ensure even distribution.

Tempering the Chocolate:

To achieve a shiny surface and firm texture, cool the chocolate mixture by stirring to about 28°C (82°F) and then warm it back up to 29-30°C (84-86°F).

Pouring and Setting:

Pour the chocolate mixture into prepared chocolate molds. Use a spatula to ensure even distribution.
Allow the chocolate to set at room temperature, which can take 1-2 hours depending on the ambient temperature.

Serving:

Once the chocolate is set, release it from the molds and break or cut into pieces.

Vanilla Cashew Bliss combines the gentle sweetness of vanilla with the nutty texture of cashews in a creamy vegan milk chocolate. This creation is a gentle indulgence that pampers the senses and invites daydreaming.

Vanilla Cashew Bliss adds a rich depth of flavor to vegan milk chocolate, with vanilla providing an aromatic experience and cashews adding a pleasant crunch. This chocolate creation is perfect for those who appreciate classic flavor combinations with a special twist.

Tropical Lime Dream - Kaffir Lime Leaves & Mango

Ingredients:

200g cocoa butter
60g rice milk powder (or other vegan milk powder)
120g powdered sugar (vegan)
2 tsp finely chopped kaffir lime leaves (use fresh for more intense flavor or dried)
100g mango, fresh or freeze-dried, finely chopped
A pinch of salt

Preparing the Ingredients:

If using fresh mango, slice the flesh from the stone and chop into fine pieces. If using freeze-dried mango, break or cut it into smaller pieces.
Wash and very finely chop the kaffir lime leaves. If using fresh leaves, briefly blanch them in hot water to intensify the aroma and soften them.

Melting Cocoa Butter:

Break the cocoa butter into small pieces and melt it over a water bath at about 40-42°C (104-108°F), stirring constantly for an even melt.

Incorporating Dry Ingredients:

Once the cocoa butter is melted, remove the vessel from the water bath. Sift in the powdered sugar and rice milk powder and stir until the mixture is smooth.

Adding Flavors:

Add the chopped kaffir lime leaves to the chocolate mixture and stir thoroughly to distribute the flavors evenly.
Stir in the finely chopped mango and mix carefully to ensure even distribution. Add a pinch of salt to balance the flavor notes.

Tempering the Chocolate:

To achieve optimal texture and shine, cool the chocolate mixture by stirring to about 26-27°C (79-81°F) and then warm it back up to 28-29°C (82-84°F).

Pouring and Setting:

Pour the chocolate mixture into prepared chocolate molds. Use a spatula to ensure even distribution.
Allow the chocolate to set at room temperature, which can take 1-2 hours depending on the ambient temperature.

Serving:

Once the chocolate is set, release it from the molds and break or cut into pieces.

Tropical Lime Dream is an exquisite blend of the exotic freshness of kaffir lime leaves and the sweet, juicy mango enveloped in creamy white chocolate. This creation captures the taste of the tropics and provides an unparalleled taste experience.

Tropical Lime Dream invites you to dive into a world of exotic flavors. The combination of mango and kaffir lime leaves in white chocolate creates an irresistible experience that both invigorates the senses and delights the palate. A true feast for lovers of exotic tastes.

Green Tea Time - Matcha & Pistachio

Ingredients:

200g cocoa mass
100g cocoa butter
100g fine cane sugar
2-3 tsp matcha powder, depending on taste preference
100g pistachios, unsalted and chopped
A pinch of salt

Preparing the Ingredients:

Coarsely chop the pistachios. Make sure to use unsalted pistachios to not compromise the flavor.

Melting Cocoa Butter and Cocoa Mass:

Break the cocoa butter and cocoa mass into smaller pieces and melt them over a water bath at a temperature of about 40-45°C (104-113°F), stirring constantly to ensure an even melt.

Stirring in Sugar and Matcha:

Remove the chocolate mixture from the water bath and stir in the cane sugar and matcha powder until well mixed and the sugar is completely dissolved. Adjust the amount of matcha powder based on the desired intensity.

Adding Pistachios:

Add the chopped pistachios to the chocolate mixture and stir gently to ensure even distribution.

Tempering the Chocolate:

To achieve optimal consistency and shine, cool the chocolate mixture by stirring to about 28°C (82°F) and then warm it back up to 31-32°C (88-90°F).

Pouring and Setting:

Pour the chocolate mixture into prepared chocolate molds. Use a spatula to ensure even distribution.
Allow the chocolate to set at room temperature, which can take 1-2 hours depending on the ambient temperature.

Serving:

Once the chocolate is set, release it from the molds and break or cut into pieces.

Green Tea Time combines the earthy depth of matcha with the nutty crunch of pistachios in a luxurious dark chocolate. A creation that opens up unique flavor worlds and can be enjoyed at any time of the day.

Green Tea Time offers an exquisite combination of the rich flavors of matcha and the crunchy texture of pistachios, perfectly embedded in the richness of dark vegan chocolate. This creation is ideal for lovers of matcha and those seeking a unique flavor combination.

Rosemary Fig Feast - Fig & Rosemary

Ingredients:

150g cocoa mass
100g cocoa butter
50g soy milk powder (or other vegan milk powder)
100g fine cane sugar
100g figs, fresh or dried, finely chopped
1-2 tsp fresh rosemary, finely chopped
A pinch of salt

Preparing the Ingredients:

If using fresh figs, wash them, remove the stem, and finely chop the flesh.
For dried figs, cut them directly into small cubes.
Thoroughly wash, dry, and finely chop the rosemary.

Melting Cocoa Butter and Cocoa Mass:

Break the cocoa butter and cocoa mass into small pieces and melt them over a water bath at about 40-45°C (104-113°F), stirring constantly to ensure an even melt.

Incorporating Milk Powder and Sugar:

Remove the chocolate mixture from the water bath and stir in the soy milk powder and cane sugar until well mixed and the sugar is completely dissolved.

Adding Flavors:

Add the chopped figs and chopped rosemary to the chocolate mixture. Stir thoroughly to ensure even distribution of ingredients and flavors. Add a pinch of salt to balance the taste notes.

Tempering the Chocolate:

To achieve optimal texture and shine, cool the chocolate mixture by stirring to about 28°C (82°F) and then warm it back up to 29-30°C (84-86°F).

Pouring and Setting:

Pour the chocolate mixture into prepared chocolate molds. Use a spatula to ensure even distribution.
Allow the chocolate to set at room temperature, which can take 1-2 hours depending on the ambient temperature.

Serving:

Once the chocolate is set, release it from the molds and break or cut into pieces.

Rosemary Fig Feast offers a harmonious combination of the natural sweetness of figs and the aromatic depth of rosemary, embedded in the creaminess of vegan milk chocolate. This creation is both rustic and sophisticated, inviting enjoyment.

Rosemary Fig Feast celebrates flavors, presenting traditional ingredients in a new light. This vegan milk chocolate is an ideal choice for those who appreciate unique flavor combinations and crave a special taste experience.

Saffron Orange Shine - Saffron & Orange

Ingredients:

200g cocoa butter
60g cashew milk powder (or other vegan milk powder)
120g powdered sugar (vegan)
Zest of 1 organic orange
2 tbsp freshly squeezed orange juice
1/4 tsp saffron threads, lightly crushed
A pinch of salt

Preparing the Ingredients:

Thoroughly wash the orange and zest the peel to obtain the zest, ensuring to use only the outer, colored part to avoid bitterness.
Squeeze the orange to extract the juice.
Lightly crush the saffron threads with your fingers to release their aroma.

Melting Cocoa Butter:

Break the cocoa butter into small pieces and melt it over a water bath at about 40-42°C (104-108°F). Ensure the water does not boil to prevent overheating.

Incorporating Dry Ingredients and Flavors:

Once the cocoa butter is melted, remove the vessel from the water bath. Sift in the powdered sugar and cashew milk powder and stir until the mixture is smooth.
Add the orange zest, orange juice, and saffron threads. Stir well to evenly distribute the flavors. Add a pinch of salt to balance the taste notes.

Tempering the Chocolate:

To achieve optimal texture and shine, cool the chocolate mixture by stirring to about 26-27°C (79-81°F) and then warm it back up to 28-29°C (82-84°F).

Pouring and Setting:

Pour the chocolate mixture into prepared chocolate molds. Use a spatula to ensure even distribution.
Allow the chocolate to set at room temperature, which can take 1-2 hours depending on the ambient temperature.

Serving:

Once the chocolate is set, release it from the molds and break or cut into pieces.

Saffron Orange Shine is an exquisite vegan white chocolate that combines the delicate aroma of saffron with the fresh citrus note of orange. This creation exudes luxury and elegance and can be enjoyed on special occasions.

Saffron Orange Shine blends the noble flavors of saffron and orange in a harmonious composition, nestled in the creaminess of white chocolate. This creation is not only a taste highlight but also a visual feast for the eyes, perfect for those seeking an extraordinary chocolate experience.

Cherry Chia Wonder - Cherry & Chia Seeds

Ingredients:

200g cocoa mass
100g cocoa butter
100g fine cane sugar
100g cherries, fresh or freeze-dried, finely chopped
2 tbsp chia seeds
A pinch of salt

Preparing the Ingredients:

If using fresh cherries, wash, pit, and finely chop them. For an intensified flavor, the cherries can be marinated in some sugar beforehand. If using freeze-dried cherries, break them into smaller pieces.
Prepare the chia seeds. Set aside some seeds for an aesthetic finish to sprinkle on the chocolate before it sets.

Melting Cocoa Butter and Cocoa Mass:

Break the cocoa butter and cocoa mass into small pieces and melt them over a water bath at about 40-45°C (104-113°F), stirring constantly to ensure an even melt.

Stirring in Sugar:

Remove the chocolate mixture from the water bath and stir in the cane sugar until well mixed and the sugar is completely dissolved.

Adding Cherries and Chia Seeds:

Add the chopped cherries and chia seeds to the chocolate mixture and stir thoroughly to ensure even distribution of the ingredients. Add a pinch of salt to balance the flavor notes.

Tempering the Chocolate:

To achieve a glossy surface and firm texture, cool the chocolate mixture by stirring to about 28°C (82°F) and then warm it back up to 31-32°C (88-90°F).

Pouring and Setting:

Pour the chocolate mixture into prepared chocolate molds. Use a spatula to ensure even distribution. Sprinkle the surface of each chocolate bar with some of the reserved chia seeds for a decorative finish.
Allow the chocolate to set at room temperature, which can take 1-2 hours depending on the ambient temperature.

Serving:

Once the chocolate is set, release it from the molds and break or cut into pieces.

Cherry Chia Wonder combines the juicy sweetness of cherries with the crunchy kick of chia seeds in rich dark chocolate. This creation offers a fascinating texture and deep flavor.

Cherry Chia Wonder is a unique blend of sweet, juicy cherries and nutritious chia seeds, enveloped in the intensity of dark chocolate. This vegan chocolate creation is perfect for those seeking a balance of flavor and healthy indulgence. A true taste wonder that delights with every bite.

Autumn Magic - Pumpkin Spice & Pecan

Ingredients:

150g cocoa mass
100g cocoa butter
50g almond milk powder (or other vegan milk powder)
100g fine cane sugar
2 tsp Pumpkin Spice (a blend of cinnamon, nutmeg, ginger, and cloves)
100g pecans, roasted and coarsely chopped
A pinch of salt

Preparing the Ingredients:

Spread the pecans on a baking sheet and roast at 180°C (356°F) for about 8-10 minutes until aromatic. After cooling, coarsely chop them.

Melting Cocoa Butter and Cocoa Mass:

Break the cocoa butter and cocoa mass into small pieces and melt them in a water bath at about 40-45°C (104-113°F), stirring constantly to ensure an even melt.

Incorporating Milk Powder and Sugar:

Remove the chocolate mixture from the water bath and stir in the almond milk powder and cane sugar until well mixed and the sugar is completely dissolved.

Adding Spices:

Add the Pumpkin Spice mixture to the chocolate mixture. Stir thoroughly to ensure an even distribution of the spices.

Adding Pecans:

Add the roasted and chopped pecans to the chocolate mixture and stir gently to ensure even distribution.

Tempering the Chocolate:

To achieve a glossy surface and firm texture, cool the chocolate mixture by stirring to about 28°C (82°F) and then warm it back up to 29-30°C (84-86°F).

Pouring and Setting:

Pour the chocolate mixture into prepared chocolate molds. Use a spatula to ensure even distribution.
Allow the chocolate to set at room temperature, which can take 1-2 hours depending on the ambient temperature.

Serving:

Once the chocolate is set, release it from the molds and break or cut into pieces.

Autumn Magic captures the essence of autumnal spices and the crunchy texture of pecans in creamy vegan milk chocolate. A perfect combination for cool days.

Autumn Magic offers a warm, spicy flavor explosion that is ideal for the autumn season. The combination of Pumpkin Spice and pecans in vegan milk chocolate creates an irresistible taste experience that invites a cozy afternoon by the fireplace. This delightful treat is perfect for those who enjoy rich, flavorful chocolates with a seasonal twist.

Minty Berry Dreams - Peppermint & Raspberry

Ingredients:

200g cocoa butter
60g almond milk powder (or other vegan milk powder)
120g powdered sugar (vegan)
2 tsp peppermint extract
100g raspberries, fresh or freeze-dried, finely chopped
A pinch of salt

Preparing the Ingredients:

If using fresh raspberries, wash and thoroughly dry them, then finely chop. For freeze-dried raspberries, chop them directly but carefully to avoid turning them into powder.

Melting Cocoa Butter:

Break the cocoa butter into small pieces and melt it over a water bath at about 40-42°C (104-108°F). Ensure the water does not boil to prevent overheating.

Incorporating Dry Ingredients:

Once the cocoa butter is melted, remove the vessel from the water bath. Sift in the powdered sugar and almond milk powder and stir until the mixture is smooth.

Adding Flavors:

Add the peppermint extract and stir thoroughly to distribute the flavors evenly. Add a pinch of salt to balance the flavor notes.

Adding Raspberries:

Gently stir the chopped raspberries into the chocolate mixture to ensure even distribution without crushing the berries too much.

Tempering the Chocolate:

To achieve optimal texture and shine, cool the chocolate mixture by stirring to about 26-27°C (79-81°F) and then warm it back up to 28-29°C (82-84°F).

Pouring and Setting:

Pour the chocolate mixture into prepared chocolate molds. Use a spatula to ensure even distribution.
Allow the chocolate to set at room temperature, which can take 1-2 hours depending on the ambient temperature.

Serving:

Once the chocolate is set, release it from the molds and break or cut into pieces.

Minty Berry Dreams combines the refreshing clarity of peppermint with the sweet tartness of raspberries in delicate white chocolate. A perfect creation for lovers of fresh, vibrant flavor profiles.

Minty Berry Dreams is a refreshing and light flavor combination, ideal for the warmer months or as a festive treat. The blend of the coolness of mint and the sweetness of raspberries makes this white chocolate an unforgettable experience.

Turmeric Coconut Fusion - Turmeric & Coconut

Ingredients:

200g cocoa mass
100g cocoa butter
100g fine cane sugar
2-3 tsp turmeric powder, depending on desired intensity
50g unsweetened coconut flakes
A pinch of salt
A few drops of coconut oil (optional, for additional smoothness)

Preparing the Ingredients:

Prepare the coconut flakes. For a more intense flavor, you can lightly toast the coconut flakes in a dry pan over low heat until they are golden brown. Let them cool afterward.

Melting Cocoa Butter and Cocoa Mass:

Break the cocoa butter and cocoa mass into small pieces and melt them over a water bath at about 40-45°C (104-113°F), stirring constantly to ensure an even melt.

Stirring in Sugar:

Remove the chocolate mixture from the water bath and stir in the cane sugar until well mixed and the sugar is completely dissolved.

Adding Turmeric and Coconut:

Add the turmeric powder and coconut flakes to the chocolate mixture. If using, add a few drops of coconut oil to make the chocolate smoother. Stir thoroughly to ensure even distribution of the ingredients. Add a pinch of salt to balance the flavor notes.

Tempering the Chocolate:

To achieve a glossy surface and firm texture, cool the chocolate mixture by stirring to about 28°C (82°F) and then warm it back up to 31-32°C (88-90°F).

Pouring and Setting:

Pour the chocolate mixture into prepared chocolate molds. Use a spatula to ensure even distribution.
Allow the chocolate to set at room temperature, which can take 1-2 hours depending on the ambient temperature.

Serving:

Once the chocolate is set, release it from the molds and break or cut into pieces.

Turmeric Coconut Fusion offers an exquisite blend of the earthy warmth of turmeric and the tropical sweetness of coconut, enveloped by the depth of dark chocolate. This creation invigorates the senses and invites you on a flavorful journey of discovery.

Turmeric Coconut Fusion is a dark chocolate creation that combines the flavor and health benefits of turmeric with the creamy texture and sweet aroma of coconut. This combination creates an unforgettable taste experience that is both innovative and deeply rooted in the tradition of culinary experimentation. Perfect for those seeking a unique and health-conscious chocolate indulgence.

Citrus Herb Delight - Tangerine & Thyme

Ingredients:

150g cocoa mass
100g cocoa butter
50g hazelnut milk powder (or other vegan milk powder)
100g fine cane sugar
Zest from 2 organic tangerines
2 tbsp freshly squeezed tangerine juice
1 tsp fresh thyme, finely chopped
A pinch of salt

Preparing the Ingredients:

Thoroughly wash the tangerines and zest the skin to obtain the zest, ensuring only to use the colored part of the skin to avoid bitterness.
Squeeze the tangerines to extract the juice.
Wash, dry, and finely chop the thyme.

Melting Cocoa Butter and Cocoa Mass:

Break the cocoa butter and cocoa mass into small pieces and melt them over a water bath at about 40-45°C (104-113°F), stirring constantly to ensure an even melt.

Incorporating Milk Powder and Sugar:

Remove the chocolate mixture from the water bath and stir in the hazelnut milk powder and cane sugar until well mixed and the sugar is completely dissolved.

Adding Flavors:

Add the tangerine zest, tangerine juice, and chopped thyme to the chocolate mixture. Stir thoroughly to ensure even distribution of flavors. Add a pinch of salt to balance the flavor notes.

Tempering the Chocolate:

To achieve a glossy surface and firm texture, cool the chocolate mixture by stirring to about 28°C (82°F) and then warm it back up to 29-30°C (84-86°F).

Pouring and Setting:

Pour the chocolate mixture into prepared chocolate molds. Use a spatula to ensure even distribution.
Allow the chocolate to set at room temperature, which can take 1-2 hours depending on the ambient temperature.

Serving:

Once the chocolate is set, release it from the molds and break or cut into pieces.

Citrus Herb Delight offers a refreshing combination of the sweetness of tangerine and the earthy note of thyme in creamy vegan milk chocolate. This creation is a homage to Mediterranean flavors and offers a unique taste experience.

Citrus Herb Delight captures the essence of sunny days and combines it with the richness of vegan milk chocolate. The mix of fresh citrus and herbal notes makes this chocolate a remarkable indulgence for those seeking new taste experiences. Perfect for a sophisticated treat or as a unique gift for chocolate connoisseurs.

Ginger Peach Kick - Ginger & Peach

Ingredients:

200g cocoa butter
60g rice milk powder (or other vegan milk powder)
120g powdered sugar (vegan)
2 tbsp fresh ginger, finely grated
100g peaches, fresh or freeze-dried, finely chopped
A pinch of salt

Preparing the Ingredients:

If using fresh peaches, wash, pit, and finely chop them. The pieces should be small enough to ensure even distribution in the chocolate. If using freeze-dried peaches, prepare them accordingly.
Peel and finely grate the ginger.

Melting Cocoa Butter:

Break the cocoa butter into small pieces and melt it over a water bath at about 40-42°C (104-108°F), stirring constantly to ensure an even melt.

Incorporating Dry Ingredients:

Once the cocoa butter is melted, remove the vessel from the water bath. Sift in the powdered sugar and rice milk powder and stir until the mixture is smooth.

Adding Flavors:

Add the grated ginger and stir thoroughly to distribute the flavors evenly. Add a pinch of salt to balance the flavor notes.

Adding Peaches:

Stir in the chopped peaches gently to ensure even distribution without crushing the fruit pieces.

Tempering the Chocolate:

To achieve optimal texture and shine, cool the chocolate mixture by stirring to about 26-27°C (79-81°F) and then warm it back up to 28-29°C (82-84°F).

Pouring and Setting:

Pour the chocolate mixture into prepared chocolate molds. Use a spatula to ensure even distribution.
Allow the chocolate to set at room temperature, which can take 1-2 hours depending on the ambient temperature.

Serving:

Once the chocolate is set, release it from the molds and break or cut into pieces.

Ginger Peach Kick offers an exciting combination of the sharpness of ginger and the sweetness of peaches in a velvety white chocolate. This creation surprises and delights with every bite.

Ginger Peach Kick introduces an exciting flavor diversity into the world of white vegan chocolate, ideal for those who appreciate a combination of sweet and spicy notes. The freshness of the peach and the spicy kick of the ginger make this chocolate an unforgettable taste experience, perfect for those looking for a unique and invigorating chocolate delight.

Maple Autumn Delight - Maple & Pecan

Ingredients:

200g cocoa mass
100g cocoa butter
100g fine cane sugar
50ml maple syrup
100g pecans, roasted and coarsely chopped
A pinch of salt

Preparing the Ingredients:

Spread the pecans on a baking sheet and roast at 180°C (356°F) for about 8-10 minutes until they are aromatic and slightly browned. After cooling, coarsely chop them.

Melting Cocoa Butter and Cocoa Mass:

Break the cocoa butter and cocoa mass into small pieces and melt them over a water bath at about 40-45°C (104-113°F), stirring constantly to ensure an even melt.

Incorporating Sugar and Maple Syrup:

Remove the chocolate mixture from the water bath and stir in the cane sugar and maple syrup until well mixed and the sugar is completely dissolved. The maple syrup adds additional depth and sweetness to the chocolate.

Adding Pecans:

Add the roasted and chopped pecans to the chocolate mixture and stir gently to ensure even distribution. Add a pinch of salt to enhance the flavor notes.

Tempering the Chocolate:

To achieve a glossy surface and firm texture, cool the chocolate mixture by stirring to about 28°C (82°F) and then warm it back up to 31-32°C (88-90°F).

Pouring and Setting:

Pour the chocolate mixture into prepared chocolate molds. Use a spatula to ensure even distribution.
Allow the chocolate to set at room temperature, which can take 1-2 hours depending on the ambient temperature.

Serving:

Once the chocolate is set, release it from the molds and break or cut into pieces.

Maple Autumn Delight offers a rich combination of natural sweetness from maple syrup and the nutty texture of pecans, embedded in the depth of dark chocolate. This perfect chocolate creation for cooler days warms the heart.

Maple Autumn Delight captures the essence of autumn flavors in a single bar of chocolate. The combination of maple syrup and pecans in dark chocolate creates an irresistible taste experience reminiscent of cozy afternoons by the fireplace.

Blueberry Lemon Freshness - Blueberry & Lemon

Ingredients:

150g cocoa mass
100g cocoa butter
50g coconut milk powder (or other vegan milk powder)
100g fine cane sugar
Zest of 1 organic lemon
2 tablespoons fresh lemon juice
100g blueberries, fresh or freeze-dried, finely chopped
A pinch of salt

Preparing the Ingredients:

Thoroughly wash the lemon and grate the zest, ensuring only the colored part of the peel is used to avoid bitterness.
Squeeze the lemon to obtain the juice.
If using fresh blueberries, wash and dry them thoroughly. If using freeze-dried blueberries, prepare them for use directly.

Melting Cocoa Butter and Cocoa Mass:

Break the cocoa butter and cocoa mass into small pieces and melt them over a water bath at about 40-45°C (104-113°F), stirring constantly to ensure an even melt.

Incorporating Milk Powder and Sugar:

Remove the chocolate mixture from the water bath and stir in the coconut milk powder and cane sugar until well combined and the sugar is completely dissolved.

Adding Flavors:

Add the lemon zest and lemon juice to the chocolate mixture and stir thoroughly to distribute the flavors evenly. Add a pinch of salt to balance the flavor notes.

74

Incorporating Blueberries:

Gently stir the blueberries into the chocolate mixture to ensure even distribution without crushing the fruit.

Tempering the Chocolate:

To achieve an optimal texture and shine, cool the chocolate mixture by stirring to about 28°C (82°F) and then warm it back up to 29-30°C (84-86°F).

Pouring and Setting:

Pour the chocolate mixture into prepared chocolate molds. Use a spatula to ensure even distribution.
Allow the chocolate to set at room temperature, which can take 1-2 hours depending on the ambient temperature.

Serving:

Once the chocolate is set, release it from the molds and break or cut into pieces.

Blueberry Lemon Freshness combines the sweetness of blueberries with the zesty freshness of lemon in creamy vegan milk chocolate. This creation is a refreshing treat that invigorates the senses.

Blueberry Lemon Freshness offers a harmonious flavor combination, perfect for the warmer months or as a bright note during the cooler season. The blend of fruity blueberries and lemony zest makes this chocolate an unforgettable taste experience.

Apricot Grain Magic - Apricot & Amaranth

Ingredients:

200g cocoa butter
60g soy milk powder (or other vegan milk powder)
120g vegan powdered sugar
100g dried apricots, finely chopped
50g puffed amaranth
A pinch of salt

Preparing the Ingredients:

Chop the dried apricots into small pieces to ensure even distribution within the chocolate.
If not using pre-puffed amaranth, prepare it according to the instructions, or use ready-puffed amaranth.

Melting Cocoa Butter:

Break the cocoa butter into small pieces and melt over a water bath at approximately 40-42°C (104-107°F), stirring constantly to ensure even melting.

Incorporating Dry Ingredients:

Once the cocoa butter is melted, remove the vessel from the water bath. Sift in the powdered sugar and soy milk powder, stirring until the mixture is smooth.

Adding Flavors:

Add the chopped apricots and puffed amaranth to the chocolate mixture. Gently stir to ensure even distribution.

Tempering the Chocolate:

To achieve optimal texture and shine, cool the chocolate mixture by stirring to about 26-27°C (79-81°F) and then warm it back up to 28-29°C (82-84°F).

Pouring and Setting:

Pour the chocolate mixture into prepared chocolate molds. Use a spatel to ensure even distribution.
Allow the chocolate to set at room temperature, which can take 1-2 hours depending on the ambient temperature.

Serving:

Once the chocolate is set, release it from the molds and break or cut into pieces.

Apricot Grain Magic combines the natural sweetness of apricots with the crispy kick of puffed amaranth in a smooth white chocolate. This creation is a fine balance of fruitiness and texture that invites enjoyment.

Apricot Grain Magic offers a flavorful composition that merges the sweet and fruity notes of apricots with the interesting crunch of amaranth in creamy white chocolate. Ideal for those seeking a chocolate with a unique texture and an exceptional flavor profile.

Apple Cinnamon Warmth - Apple & Cinnamon

Ingredients:

200g cocoa mass
100g cocoa butter
100g fine cane sugar
2 tsp cinnamon powder
100g dried apples, finely chopped
A pinch of salt

Preparing the Ingredients:

Chop the dried apples into small, bite-sized pieces. For a finer texture, the pieces can be further crushed according to preference.

Melting Cocoa Butter and Cocoa Mass:

Break the cocoa butter and cocoa mass into small pieces and melt them over a water bath at approximately 40-45°C (104-113°F), stirring constantly to ensure even melting.

Incorporating Sugar and Cinnamon:

Remove the chocolate mixture from the water bath and stir in the cane sugar and cinnamon powder until well mixed and the sugar is completely dissolved.

Adding Apples:

Add the chopped dried apples to the chocolate mixture and stir gently to ensure even distribution.

Tempering the Chocolate:

To achieve a shiny surface and a firm texture, cool the chocolate mixture by stirring to about 28°C (82°F) and then heat it back up to 31-32°C (88-90°F).

Pouring and Setting:

Pour the chocolate mixture into prepared chocolate molds. Use a spatula to ensure even distribution.
Allow the chocolate to set at room temperature, which can take 1-2 hours depending on the ambient temperature.

Serving:

Once the chocolate has set, release it from the molds and break or cut into pieces.

Apple Cinnamon Warmth offers a delicious combination of the natural sweetness of apples and the spicy warmth of cinnamon, embedded in the richness of dark chocolate. A perfect chocolate creation for cozy evenings.

Apple Cinnamon Warmth is a warm invitation to enjoy the pleasures of the colder seasons. This dark vegan chocolate combines the classic flavors of apple and cinnamon into a flavorful experience that both comforts and indulges. Ideal for lovers of spiced chocolate and those seeking a touch of coziness in their chocolate selection.

Morning Crunch - Granola-Crunch

Ingredients:

150g cocoa mass
100g cocoa butter
50g oat milk powder (or other vegan milk powder)
100g fine cane sugar
150g granola (preferably sugar-free, may include nuts, seeds, and dried fruits)
A pinch of salt

Preparing the Ingredients:

Choose a sugar-free granola to better control the flavor and sweetness. The granola can include nuts, seeds, and dried fruits based on personal preference.

Melting Cocoa Butter and Cocoa Mass:

Break the cocoa butter and cocoa mass into small pieces and melt them in a water bath at about 40-45°C (104-113°F), stirring constantly for even melting.

Incorporating Milk Powder and Sugar:

Remove the chocolate mixture from the water bath and stir in the oat milk powder and cane sugar until well mixed and the sugar is completely dissolved.

Adding Granola:

Stir the granola into the chocolate mixture carefully to ensure even distribution. Make sure the mixture is well combined so that granola is found in every piece of chocolate.

Tempering the Chocolate:

To achieve a shiny surface and a firm texture, cool the chocolate mixture by stirring to about 28°C (82°F) and then heat it back up to 29-30°C (84-86°F).

Pouring and Setting:

Pour the chocolate mixture into prepared molds. Use a spatula to ensure even distribution.
Allow the chocolate to set at room temperature, which can take 1-2 hours depending on the ambient temperature.

Serving:

Once the chocolate has set, release it from the molds and break or cut into pieces.

Morning Crunch offers a delightful combination of creamy vegan milk chocolate and the crunchy bite of granola. A perfect chocolate creation for starting the day or as an energy-rich snack.

Morning Crunch is a flavorful and texture-rich chocolate creation that combines the creaminess of vegan milk chocolate with the crunchy delight of granola. Ideal for those looking for a tasty and filling chocolate that serves well as both a breakfast and a snack.

Coconut Paradies - Coconut & Pineapple

Ingredients:

200g cocoa butter
60g coconut milk powder (or other vegan milk powder)
120g vegan powdered sugar
100g dried pineapple, finely chopped
50g unsweetened coconut flakes
A pinch of salt

Preparing the Ingredients:

Select dried pineapple pieces and chop them into smaller pieces to ensure even distribution in the chocolate.
Prepare the coconut flakes. For a more intense coconut flavor, lightly toast the flakes in a dry pan until golden brown, then let cool.

Melting Cocoa Butter:

Break the cocoa butter into small pieces and melt over a water bath at approximately 40-42°C (104-107°F), ensuring the water does not boil to prevent overheating.

Incorporating Dry Ingredients:

Once the cocoa butter is melted, remove from the water bath. Sift in the powdered sugar and coconut milk powder, stirring until the mixture is smooth.

Adding Flavors:

Add the chopped pineapple and coconut flakes to the chocolate mixture. Stir gently to ensure even distribution. Add a pinch of salt to balance the flavors.

Tempering the Chocolate:

To achieve optimal texture and shine, cool the chocolate mixture by stirring to about 26-27°C (79-81°F) and then reheat to 28-29°C (82-84°F).

Pouring and Setting:

Pour the chocolate mixture into prepared molds. Use a spatula to ensure even distribution.
Allow the chocolate to set at room temperature, which may take 1-2 hours depending on the ambient temperature.

Serving:

Once the chocolate has set, release it from the molds and break or cut into pieces.

Coconut Paradies transports you to an exotic world with each bite. The combination of sweet pineapple and rich coconut flavor in delicate white chocolate creates an unforgettable taste experience.

Coconut Paradies is a flavorful tribute to the tropics that invigorates the senses and leaves you craving more. This white vegan chocolate is perfect for those looking for a sweet escape to exotic locales.

Cardamom Fusion - Cardamom & Almond

Ingredients:

200g cocoa mass
100g cocoa butter
100g fine cane sugar
1-2 tsp cardamom powder, to taste
100g almonds, roasted and coarsely chopped
A pinch of salt

Preparing the Ingredients:

Spread the almonds on a baking sheet and roast at 180°C (356°F) for about 8-10 minutes until they are lightly browned and fragrant. After cooling, coarsely chop them.

Melting Cocoa Butter and Cocoa Mass:

Break the cocoa butter and cocoa mass into small pieces and melt them over a water bath at a temperature of about 40-45°C (104-113°F). Constant stirring ensures an even melt.

Incorporating Sugar and Cardamom:

Remove the chocolate mixture from the water bath and stir in the cane sugar and cardamom powder until everything is well mixed and the sugar is completely dissolved. Adjust the amount of cardamom powder according to your taste preference.

Adding Almonds:

Add the roasted and chopped almonds to the chocolate mixture and stir gently to ensure an even distribution.

Tempering the Chocolate:

To achieve a glossy surface and a firm texture, cool the chocolate mixture by stirring to about 28°C (82°F) and then reheat it to 31-32°C (88-90°F).

Pouring and Setting:

Pour the chocolate mixture into prepared molds. Use a spatel to ensure even distribution.
Allow the chocolate to set at room temperature, which may take 1-2 hours depending on the ambient temperature.

Serving:

Once the chocolate has set, release it from the molds and break or cut into pieces.

Cardamom Fusion offers an exquisite combination of the spicy warmth of cardamom and the nutty crunch of almonds, embedded in the richness of dark chocolate. A perfect chocolate creation for lovers of exotic spices.

Cardamom Fusion is a tribute to the rich flavors and textures that the culinary world has to offer. This dark vegan chocolate is ideal for those seeking a complex taste experience that both invigorates and indulges the palate.

Autumnal Cinnamon Apple - Apple & Cinnamon

Ingredients:

150g cocoa mass
100g cocoa butter
50g oat milk powder (or other vegan milk powder)
100g fine cane sugar
100g apples, fresh or dried, finely diced
2 tsp cinnamon powder
A pinch of salt

Preparing the Ingredients:

If using fresh apples, wash, core, and finely dice them. For a more intense flavor, the apple pieces can be marinated beforehand with some cinnamon and sugar. If using dried apples, cut them directly into small dice.

Melting Cocoa Butter and Cocoa Mass:

Break the cocoa butter and cocoa mass into small pieces and melt them over a water bath at about 40-45°C (104-113°F), stirring constantly to ensure even melting.

Incorporating Milk Powder and Sugar:

Remove the chocolate mixture from the water bath and stir in the oat milk powder and cane sugar until everything is well mixed and the sugar is completely dissolved.

Adding Apple and Cinnamon:

Add the apple dice and cinnamon powder to the chocolate mixture. Stir thoroughly to ensure an even distribution of ingredients. Add a pinch of salt to balance the flavors.

Tempering the Chocolate:

To achieve optimal texture and shine, cool the chocolate mixture by stirring to about 28°C (82°F) and then heat it again to 29-30°C (84-86°F).

Pouring and Setting:

Pour the chocolate mixture into prepared molds. Use a spatula to ensure even distribution.
Allow the chocolate to set at room temperature, which can take 1-2 hours depending on the ambient temperature.

Serving:

Once the chocolate has set, release it from the molds and break or cut into pieces.

Autumnal Cinnamon Apple combines the cozy warmth of cinnamon with the fresh sweetness of apples in a velvety vegan milk chocolate. This creation captures the essence of autumn and invites enjoyment.

Autumnal Cinnamon Apple is a loving tribute to the flavors that define autumn. This vegan milk chocolate is the perfect comfort for cool days, offering a piece of warmth and coziness that one can indulge in at any time.

Rhubarb Vanilla Bliss - Rhubarb & Vanilla

Ingredients:

200g cocoa butter
60g almond milk powder (or other vegan milk powder)
120g powdered sugar (vegan)
100g rhubarb, fresh or freeze-dried, chopped into small pieces
1 vanilla pod, seeds scraped out (or 2 tsp vanilla extract)
A pinch of salt

Preparing the Ingredients:

If using fresh rhubarb, wash it and cut into small, about 1 cm pieces. To soften the acidity, you can marinate the rhubarb with some sugar beforehand. If using freeze-dried rhubarb, use it directly.
Split the vanilla pod lengthwise and scrape out the seeds with the back of a knife.

Melting Cocoa Butter:

Break the cocoa butter into small pieces and melt over a water bath at about 40-42°C (104-107°F), stirring constantly to ensure even melting.

Incorporating Dry Ingredients:

Once the cocoa butter has melted, remove the vessel from the water bath. Sift in the powdered sugar and almond milk powder and stir until the mixture is smooth.

Adding Flavors:

Add the chopped rhubarb and the vanilla seeds (or vanilla extract) to the chocolate mixture. Stir thoroughly to ensure even distribution of the ingredients. Add a pinch of salt to balance the flavors.

Tempering the Chocolate:

To achieve an optimal texture and shine, cool the chocolate mixture by stirring to about 26-27°C (79-81°F) and then heat it again to 28-29°C (82-84°F).

Pouring and Setting:

Pour the chocolate mixture into prepared molds. Use a spatula to ensure even distribution.
Allow the chocolate to set at room temperature, which can take 1-2 hours depending on the ambient temperature.

Serving:

Once the chocolate has set, release it from the molds and break or cut into pieces.

Rhubarb Vanilla Bliss combines the distinctive tartness of rhubarb with the gentle sweetness of vanilla in a creamy white chocolate. This creation evokes spring feelings with every bite.

Rhubarb Vanilla Bliss is a refreshing and comforting chocolate creation that captures the vibrant flavors of spring. The combination of rhubarb and vanilla in vegan white chocolate offers a unique taste experience reminiscent of warm days and blooming gardens. A truly blissful indulgence for all the senses.

Cherry Dream - Sour Cherry & Vanilla

Ingredients:

200g cocoa mass
100g cocoa butter
100g fine cane sugar
100g sour cherries, dried or freeze-dried, finely chopped
1 vanilla pod, seeds scraped out (or 2 tsp vanilla extract)
A pinch of salt

Preparing the Ingredients:

If using dried or freeze-dried sour cherries, chop them into small pieces to better release the flavors and ensure even distribution in the chocolate. Split the vanilla pod lengthwise and scrape out the seeds with the back of a knife.

Melting Cocoa Butter and Cocoa Mass:

Break the cocoa butter and cocoa mass into small pieces and melt them over a water bath at a temperature of about 40-45°C (104-113°F), stirring constantly to ensure even melting.

Stirring in Sugar:

Remove the chocolate mixture from the water bath and stir in the cane sugar until well mixed and the sugar is completely dissolved.

Adding Sour Cherries and Vanilla:

Add the chopped sour cherries and the vanilla seeds (or vanilla extract) to the chocolate mixture. Stir thoroughly to ensure an even distribution of the ingredients. Add a pinch of salt to enhance the flavor notes.

Tempering the Chocolate:

To achieve a glossy surface and a firm texture, cool the chocolate mixture by stirring to about 28°C (82°F) and then reheat it to 31-32°C (88-90°F).

Pouring and Setting:

Pour the chocolate mixture into prepared molds. Use a spatel to ensure even distribution.
Allow the chocolate to set at room temperature, which can take 1-2 hours depending on the ambient temperature.

Serving:

Once the chocolate has set, release it from the molds and break or cut into pieces.

Cherry Dream is an exquisite combination of the tart freshness of sour cherries and the sweet, aromatic depth of vanilla, enveloped in rich dark chocolate. A creation that masterfully captures the balance between sweetness and acidity.

Cherry Dream offers an intense flavor experience that revitalizes the senses and invites you to dream. This vegan dark chocolate is a tribute to the diversity and depth of natural flavors, a perfect choice for those looking for a memorable indulgence.

Campfire Romance - S'mores (with vegan marshmallows)

Ingredients:

150g cocoa mass
100g cocoa butter
50g coconut milk powder (or other vegan milk powder)
100g fine cane sugar
100g vegan marshmallows, chopped or torn into small pieces
100g vegan Graham crackers (or similar biscuits), coarsely crumbled
A pinch of salt

Preparation:

Cut or tear the vegan marshmallows into small pieces that will easily fit into the chocolate molds.
Crumble the Graham crackers or similar biscuits into coarse pieces, not too fine, to preserve texture.

Melting Cocoa Butter and Cocoa Mass:

Break the cocoa butter and cocoa mass into small pieces and melt them over a water bath at approximately 40-45°C (104-113°F), stirring constantly to ensure an even melt.

Stirring in Milk Powder and Sugar:

Remove the chocolate mixture from the water bath and stir in the coconut milk powder and cane sugar until well mixed and the sugar is completely dissolved.

Tempering the Chocolate:

To achieve an optimal texture and shine, cool the chocolate mixture by stirring to about 28°C (82°F) and then reheat it to 29-30°C (84-86°F).
Adding Marshmallows and Graham Crackers:

First, pour a thin layer of the tempered chocolate into the prepared chocolate molds. Then sprinkle a layer of marshmallows and Graham cracker crumbs. Pour another layer of chocolate over the top to cover the filling. Repeat this process until the molds are full, ensuring the final layer is chocolate.

Pouring and Setting:

Ensure that the chocolate mixture fills all gaps and the molds are evenly filled. Use a spatula to smooth the surface.
Allow the chocolate to set at room temperature, which can take 1-2 hours depending on the room climate.

Serving:

Once the chocolate has set, release it from the molds and break or cut it into pieces.

Campfire Romance is a nostalgic journey back to those sweet moments by the fire, captured in the creamy texture of vegan milk chocolate. The combination of melted marshmallows and crispy Graham crackers offers an unparalleled taste experience.

Campfire Romance combines the classic elements of a S'mores into a single chocolate bar. This vegan milk chocolate is a true delight for anyone who loves the combination of sweet and crispy, while reminiscing about cozy evenings under the starry sky.

Spicy Mango - Mango & Chili

Ingredients:

200g cocoa butter
60g almond milk powder (or other vegan milk powder)
120g powdered sugar (vegan)
100g mango, fresh or freeze-dried, cut into small pieces
1-2 tsp chili flakes (adjust to desired spiciness)
A pinch of salt

Preparation:

If using fresh mango, cut the flesh away from the stone and chop into fine pieces. If using freeze-dried mango, break it into smaller pieces. Prepare the chili flakes. Adjust the amount according to your taste preferences, depending on how spicy you want the chocolate to be.

Melting Cocoa Butter:

Break the cocoa butter into small pieces and melt it over a water bath at a temperature of approximately 40-42°C (104-107°F). Constant stirring ensures an even melt.

Stirring in Dry Ingredients:

Once the cocoa butter has melted, remove the vessel from the water bath. Sift in the powdered sugar and almond milk powder and stir until the mixture is smooth.

Adding Flavors:

Add the mango pieces and chili flakes to the chocolate mixture. Stir thoroughly to ensure an even distribution of the ingredients. Add a pinch of salt to enhance the flavor notes.

Tempering the Chocolate:

To achieve an optimal texture and shine, cool the chocolate mixture by stirring to about 26-27°C (79-81°F) and then reheat it to 28-29°C (82-84°F).

Pouring and Setting:

Pour the chocolate mixture into prepared chocolate molds. Use a spatel to ensure an even distribution.
Allow the chocolate to set at room temperature, which can take 1-2 hours depending on the room climate.

Serving:

Once the chocolate has set, release it from the molds and break or cut it into pieces.

Spicy Mango offers an exotic combination of the sweetness of mango and the spicy heat of chili, embedded in creamy white chocolate. A creation that invigorates the senses and invites an unforgettable taste experience.

Spicy Mango is a unique flavor creation that combines the rich sweetness of mango with a hint of heat from chili in a harmonious union with vegan white chocolate. This combination makes every chocolate bar an exciting treat for lovers of spicy and sweet flavors.

Peanut Swirl - Peanut Butter

Ingredients:

200g cocoa mass
100g cocoa butter
100g fine cane sugar
100g peanut butter, smooth or crunchy (according to preference)
A pinch of salt

Preparation:

Ensure the peanut butter is at room temperature for easier handling. Using crunchy peanut butter will add extra texture to your swirl.

Melting Cocoa Butter and Cocoa Mass:

Break the cocoa butter and cocoa mass into smaller pieces and melt them over a water bath at approximately 40-45°C (104-113°F). Constant stirring ensures an even melt.

Stirring in Sugar:

Remove the chocolate mixture from the water bath and stir in the cane sugar until well combined and the sugar is completely dissolved.

Tempering the Chocolate:

To achieve a shiny surface and a firm texture, cool the chocolate mass by stirring to about 28°C (82°F) and then reheat it to 31-32°C (88-90°F). Preparing Peanut Butter:

Gently heat the peanut butter in a pot or microwave to make it more fluid, facilitating the creation of the swirl effect.
Pouring and Adding Peanut Butter:

Pour a layer of the tempered dark chocolate into prepared chocolate molds. Then carefully spoon some dollops of peanut butter over the chocolate.

Use a toothpick or the end of a spoon to gently pull the peanut butter through the chocolate to create the swirl effect. Repeat the process until the molds are filled, with the top layer being chocolate.

Setting:

Allow the chocolate to set at room temperature, which can take 1-2 hours depending on the room climate.

Serving:

Once the chocolate has set, release it from the molds and break or cut it into pieces.

Peanut Swirl is a tantalizing combination of rich dark chocolate and creamy peanut butter, united in an elegant swirl. A creation that will delight peanut butter lovers.

Peanut Swirl combines the depth of dark chocolate with the nutty sweetness of peanut butter in an artistic swirl, impressing both in taste and appearance. This vegan chocolate creation is a true delight for anyone who appreciates the combination of chocolate and peanut butter.

Mocha Almond Delight - Mocha & Almond

Ingredients:

150g cocoa mass
100g cocoa butter
50g hazelnut milk powder (or other vegan milk powder)
100g fine cane sugar
2-3 tbsp strong espresso or mocha, cooled
100g almonds, roasted and coarsely chopped
A pinch of salt

Preparation:

Prepare a strong espresso or mocha and allow it to cool completely.
Spread the almonds on a baking sheet and roast at 180°C (356°F) for
about 8-10 minutes until they are fragrant and lightly browned. After
cooling, coarsely chop them.

Melting Cocoa Butter and Cocoa Mass:

Break the cocoa butter and cocoa mass into smaller pieces and melt them
over a water bath at approximately 40-45°C (104-113°F). Constant
stirring ensures an even melt.

Stirring in Milk Powder and Sugar:

Remove the chocolate mixture from the water bath and stir in the
hazelnut milk powder and cane sugar until well combined and the sugar
is completely dissolved.

Adding Mocha:

Add the cooled espresso or mocha to the chocolate mixture and stir
thoroughly to evenly distribute the liquid.

Tempering the Chocolate:

To achieve an optimal texture and shine, cool the chocolate mass by stirring to about 28°C (82°F) and then reheat it to 29-30°C (84-86°F).

Adding Almonds:

Sprinkle the roasted and chopped almonds over the still liquid chocolate in the molds after filling them about halfway. Then add the remaining chocolate mixture to encase the almonds.

Pouring and Setting:

Complete the filling of the chocolate molds and use a spatel to ensure an even distribution.
Allow the chocolate to set at room temperature, which can take 1-2 hours depending on the room climate.

Serving:

Once the chocolate has set, release it from the molds and break or cut it into pieces.

Mocha Almond Delight offers a rich combination of the deep flavor of mocha and the nutty texture of almonds, enveloped in creamy vegan milk chocolate. A creation that excites both coffee and chocolate lovers.

Mocha Almond Delight is a flavorful tribute to the joys of coffee and chocolate, enhanced with the crunchy bite of almonds. This vegan milk chocolate creation is perfect for those who crave a balanced, aromatic, and texture-rich tasting experience.

Blood Orange Cardamom Magic - Blood Orange & Cardamom

Ingredients:

200g cocoa butter
60g cashew milk powder (or other vegan milk powder)
120g powdered sugar (vegan)
Zest of 2 blood oranges
Juice of 1 blood orange
1 tsp cardamom powder
A pinch of salt

Preparation:

Thoroughly wash the blood oranges and then zest the skin to collect the zest. Be sure to use only the colored part of the peel to avoid bitterness. Halve the blood oranges and squeeze one to obtain the juice.

Melting Cocoa Butter:

Break the cocoa butter into small pieces and melt over a water bath at a temperature of about 40-42°C (104-107°F). Constant stirring ensures an even melt.

Stirring in Dry Ingredients:

Once the cocoa butter is melted, remove the vessel from the water bath. Sift the powdered sugar and cashew milk powder into it and stir until the mixture is smooth.

Adding Flavors:

Add the blood orange zest, blood orange juice, and cardamom powder to the chocolate mixture. Stir thoroughly to ensure even distribution of the flavors. Add a pinch of salt to enhance the flavor notes.

Tempering the Chocolate:

To achieve optimal texture and shine, cool the chocolate mass by stirring to about 26-27°C (79-81°F) and then reheat it to 28-29°C (82-84°F).

Pouring and Setting:

Pour the chocolate mixture into prepared chocolate molds. Use a spatula to ensure an even distribution.
Allow the chocolate to set at room temperature, which can take 1-2 hours depending on the room climate.

Serving:

Once the chocolate has set, release it from the molds and break or cut it into pieces.

Blood Orange Cardamom Magic combines the fresh acidity of blood oranges with the warm, aromatic notes of cardamom in a delicate white chocolate. A creation that enchants the senses with every bite.

Blood Orange Cardamom Magic is an elegant and flavorful combination that captures the delicate flavors of blood orange and cardamom in creamy white chocolate. This vegan chocolate creation offers an unparalleled taste experience, reminiscent of sunny days and exotic spice markets.

Pomegranate Power - Pomegranate & Maca

Ingredients:

200g cocoa mass
100g cocoa butter
100g fine cane sugar
100g pomegranate seeds, fresh or freeze-dried
2 tsp maca powder
A pinch of salt

Preparation:

If using fresh pomegranates, halve them and gently remove the seeds. Allow the seeds to dry on a paper towel to remove excess moisture. If using freeze-dried pomegranate seeds, use them directly.
Prepare the maca powder. Maca, known for its energy-boosting properties, adds a slightly nutty flavor.

Melting Cocoa Butter and Cocoa Mass:

Break the cocoa butter and cocoa mass into small pieces and melt them over a water bath at a temperature of about 40-45°C (104-113°F). Constant stirring ensures an even melt.

Stirring in Sugar:

Remove the chocolate mixture from the water bath and stir in the cane sugar until well mixed and the sugar is completely dissolved.

Adding Maca Powder:

Add the maca powder to the chocolate mixture and stir thoroughly to ensure even distribution. Add a pinch of salt to enhance the flavor notes.

Tempering the Chocolate:

To achieve a glossy surface and a firm texture, cool the chocolate mass by stirring to about 28°C (82°F) and then reheat it to 31-32°C (88-90°F).

Adding Pomegranate Seeds:

Sprinkle the pomegranate seeds over the still liquid chocolate in the molds after they have been half-filled. Then add the remaining chocolate mixture to enclose the seeds.

Pouring and Setting:

Complete the filling of the chocolate molds and use a spatula to ensure an even distribution.
Allow the chocolate to set at room temperature, which can take 1-2 hours depending on the room climate.

Serving:

Once the chocolate has set, release it from the molds and break or cut it into pieces.

Pomegranate Power offers a fascinating combination of the sweet and tart freshness of pomegranate seeds and the earthy note of maca in rich dark chocolate. A creation that invigorates the palate and energizes.

Pomegranate Power is a unique and powerful chocolate creation that combines the antioxidant benefits of pomegranates with the nutrient-rich properties of maca in the depth of dark chocolate. This vegan chocolate is a true delight for those seeking a sweet yet healthy indulgence.

Autumnal Sweet Potato - Sweet Potato & Maple

Ingredients:

150g cocoa mass
100g cocoa butter
50g almond milk powder (or other vegan milk powder)
100g fine cane sugar
100g sweet potato, cooked and pureed
3 tbsp maple syrup
1 tsp cinnamon powder
A pinch of salt

Preparation:

Cook a medium-sized sweet potato until soft. Let it cool, peel, and puree the flesh until smooth.
Prepare the additional ingredients: measure the maple syrup, cinnamon powder, and a pinch of salt.

Melting Cocoa Butter and Cocoa Mass:

Break the cocoa butter and cocoa mass into small pieces and melt them over a water bath at a temperature of about 40-45°C (104-113°F). Constant stirring ensures an even melt.

Stirring in Milk Powder and Sugar:

Remove the chocolate mixture from the water bath and stir in the almond milk powder and cane sugar until well mixed and the sugar is completely dissolved.

Adding Sweet Potato Puree and Flavors:

Add the sweet potato puree, maple syrup, and cinnamon powder to the chocolate mixture. Stir thoroughly to ensure even distribution of the ingredients. Add a pinch of salt to enhance the flavor notes.

Tempering the Chocolate:

To achieve optimal texture and shine, cool the chocolate mass by stirring to about 28°C (82°F) and then reheat it to 29-30°C (84-86°F).

Pouring and Setting:

Pour the chocolate mixture into prepared chocolate molds. Use a spatula to ensure even distribution.
Allow the chocolate to set at room temperature, which can take 1-2 hours depending on the room climate.

Serving:

Once the chocolate has set, release it from the molds and break or cut it into pieces.

Autumnal Sweet Potato is a warming combination of the nutty taste of sweet potato, the sweet note of maple syrup, and a hint of cinnamon, encased in creamy vegan milk chocolate. A creation that captures the essence of autumn and can be enjoyed at any time of day.

Autumnal Sweet Potato offers an unparalleled flavor experience that unites traditional autumnal flavors in a unique chocolate creation. This vegan milk chocolate is a perfect treat for those who appreciate the combination of sweet and savory notes and crave a special culinary experience.

Spicy Pumpkin - Pumpkin & Spices

Ingredients:

200g cocoa butter
60g soy milk powder (or other vegan milk powder)
120g powdered sugar (vegan)
100g pumpkin puree (from cooked and pureed pumpkin)
1 tsp Pumpkin Spice (a blend of cinnamon, nutmeg, ginger, and cloves)
A pinch of salt

Preparation:

Cook pumpkin pieces until soft. Then puree them into a smooth pumpkin puree.
Prepare the Pumpkin Spice by mixing cinnamon, nutmeg, ginger, and cloves in the specified proportions.

Melting Cocoa Butter:

Break the cocoa butter into small pieces and melt it over a water bath at a temperature of about 40-42°C (104-107°F). Constant stirring ensures an even melt.

Stirring in Dry Ingredients:

Once the cocoa butter has melted, remove the vessel from the water bath. Sift in the powdered sugar and soy milk powder and stir until the mixture is smooth.

Adding Pumpkin Puree and Spices:

Add the pumpkin puree and Pumpkin Spice to the chocolate mixture. Stir thoroughly to ensure even distribution of the ingredients. Add a pinch of salt to enhance the flavor notes.

Tempering the Chocolate:

To achieve optimal texture and shine, cool the chocolate mass by stirring to about 26-27°C (79-81°F) and then reheat it to 28-29°C (82-84°F).

Pouring and Setting:

Pour the chocolate mixture into prepared chocolate molds. Use a spatel to ensure even distribution.
Let the chocolate set at room temperature, which can take 1-2 hours depending on the room climate.

Serving:

Once the chocolate has set, release it from the molds and break or cut it into pieces.

Spiced Pumpkin is a celebratory combination of the rich taste of pumpkin and the warm embrace of autumn spices, encased in sweet vegan white chocolate. A creation that captures the coziness and magic of the autumn season.

Spiced Pumpkin offers a unique flavor experience that unites the essence of autumn in a luxurious chocolate bar. This vegan white chocolate is a tribute to seasonal flavors, ideal for those seeking a sweet indulgence with a touch of warmth and spice.

Pear Nutmeg Fusion - Pear & Nutmeg

Ingredients:

200g cocoa mass
100g cocoa butter
100g fine cane sugar
100g pears, fresh or freeze-dried, finely diced
1 tsp nutmeg, freshly grated
A pinch of salt

Preparation:

If using fresh pears, wash, core, and dice finely. For a more intense flavor, marinate the pear pieces beforehand with some cinnamon and sugar to enhance their sweetness. For dried pears, dice them directly into small cubes.
Grate the nutmeg freshly to maximize the aroma.

Melting Cocoa Butter and Cocoa Mass:

Break the cocoa butter and cocoa mass into small pieces and melt them over a water bath at a temperature of about 40-45°C (104-113°F). Constant stirring ensures an even melt.

Stirring in Sugar:

Remove the chocolate mixture from the water bath and stir in the cane sugar until everything is well mixed and the sugar has completely dissolved.

Adding Pears and Nutmeg:

Add the diced pears and freshly grated nutmeg to the chocolate mixture. Stir thoroughly to ensure an even distribution of the ingredients. Add a pinch of salt to enhance the flavor notes.

Tempering the Chocolate:

To achieve a glossy surface and firm texture, cool the chocolate mass by stirring to about 28°C (82°F) and then heat it again to 31-32°C (88-90°F).

Pouring and Setting:

Pour the chocolate mixture into prepared chocolate molds. Use a spatula to ensure an even distribution.
Let the chocolate set at room temperature, which can take 1-2 hours depending on the room climate.

Serving:

Once the chocolate has set, release it from the molds and break or cut it into pieces.

Pear Nutmeg Fusion is an exquisite combination of the natural sweetness of pears and the spicy note of nutmeg, encased in rich dark chocolate. A creation that offers a harmonious flavor explosion with each bite.

Pear Nutmeg Fusion elegantly combines the delicate flavors of pear and nutmeg in the depth of dark chocolate. This vegan chocolate creation is a tribute to the subtle pleasures of nature and offers an unforgettable flavor experience for those seeking a special culinary discovery.

Cherry Pistachio Celebration - Pistachio & Cherry

Ingredients:

150g cocoa mass
100g cocoa butter
50g rice milk powder (or other vegan milk powder)
100g fine cane sugar
100g cherries, fresh or freeze-dried, finely chopped
100g pistachios, unsalted and chopped
A pinch of salt

Preparation:

If using fresh cherries, wash, pit, and finely chop them. For a more intense flavor, marinate the cherries beforehand with some sugar. If using freeze-dried cherries, chop them directly into small pieces.
Coarsely chop the pistachios. For added flavor and texture, the pistachios can be lightly toasted.

Melting Cocoa Butter and Cocoa Mass:

Break the cocoa butter and cocoa mass into small pieces and melt them over a water bath at a temperature of about 40-45°C (104-113°F). Constant stirring ensures an even melt.

Stirring in Milk Powder and Sugar:

Remove the chocolate mixture from the water bath and stir in the rice milk powder and cane sugar until well mixed and the sugar has completely dissolved.

Adding Cherries and Pistachios:

Add the chopped cherries and pistachios to the chocolate mixture. Stir thoroughly to ensure an even distribution of the ingredients. Add a pinch of salt to enhance the flavor notes.

Tempering the Chocolate:

To achieve an optimal texture and gloss, cool the chocolate mass by stirring to about 28°C (82°F) and then heat it again to 29-30°C (84-86°F).

Pouring and Setting:

Pour the chocolate mixture into prepared chocolate molds. Use a spatula to ensure an even distribution.
Let the chocolate set at room temperature, which can take 1-2 hours depending on the room climate.

Serving:

Once the chocolate has set, release it from the molds and break or cut it into pieces.

Cherry Pistachio Celebration is a festive combination of the sweet and slightly tart notes of cherries and the nutty flavor of pistachios, encased in creamy vegan milk chocolate. A creation that invites celebration with every bite.

Cherry Pistachio Celebration offers a rich and colorful flavor experience, celebrating the joys of pistachios and cherries in a harmonious connection with vegan milk chocolate. This chocolate creation is perfect for those seeking a special and indulgent experience.

Espresso-Hazelnut Bliss - Espresso & Hazelnut

Ingredients:

200g cocoa mass
100g cocoa butter
100g fine cane sugar
2 tbsp espresso, freshly brewed and cooled
100g hazelnuts, roasted and coarsely chopped
A pinch of fine sea salt

Preparation:

Spread the hazelnuts on a baking sheet and roast at 180°C (356°F) for about 10 minutes until fragrant and lightly browned. After cooling, coarsely chop them.
Brew a strong espresso and let it cool.

Melting Cocoa Butter and Cocoa Mass:

Break the cocoa butter and cocoa mass into smaller pieces and melt them over a water bath at a temperature of about 40-45°C (104-113°F). Constant stirring ensures an even melt.

Stirring in Sugar and Espresso:

Remove the chocolate mixture from the water bath and stir in the cane sugar and cooled espresso until well mixed and the sugar is completely dissolved.

Adding Hazelnuts:

Add the roasted and chopped hazelnuts to the chocolate mixture and stir gently to ensure even distribution. Add a pinch of fine sea salt to enhance the flavor notes.

Tempering the Chocolate:

To achieve a glossy surface and firm texture, cool the chocolate mass by stirring to about 28°C (82°F) and then heat it again to 31-32°C (88-90°F).

Pouring and Setting:

Pour the chocolate mixture into prepared chocolate molds. Use a spatula to ensure even distribution.
Let the chocolate set at room temperature, which can take 1-2 hours depending on the room climate.

Serving:

Once the chocolate has set, release it from the molds and break or cut it into pieces.

Espresso-Hazelnut Bliss combines the rich depth of espresso with the crunchy texture and nutty aroma of hazelnuts in dark chocolate. An uplifting creation for coffee and chocolate lovers.

Espresso-Hazelnut Bliss is the perfect chocolate creation for anyone who enjoys the invigorating taste of espresso and the nutty sweetness of hazelnuts in the rich embrace of dark chocolate.

Pear-Gorgonzola Dream - Pear & Gorgonzola Flavor

Ingredients:

200g cocoa butter
60g almond milk powder (or other vegan milk powder)
120g powdered sugar (vegan)
100g pears, fresh or dried, finely chopped
2 tsp vegan Gorgonzola flavor (e.g., nutritional yeast flakes combined with finely ground walnuts)
A pinch of salt
Note: Since real Gorgonzola is not vegan, we use a blend of nutritional yeast flakes and finely ground walnuts to simulate a similar flavor.

Preparation:

If using fresh pears, wash, core, and finely chop them. Directly finely chop dried pears.
Prepare a mix of nutritional yeast flakes and finely ground walnuts to mimic the Gorgonzola flavor.

Melting Cocoa Butter:

Break the cocoa butter into small pieces and melt over a water bath at a temperature of about 40-42°C (104-107.6°F). Constant stirring ensures an even melt.

Stirring in Dry Ingredients:

Once the cocoa butter is melted, remove the vessel from the water bath. Sift in the powdered sugar and almond milk powder and stir until the mixture is smooth.

Adding Flavors:

Add the chopped pears and the prepared Gorgonzola mixture to the chocolate mixture. Stir gently to ensure even distribution. Add a pinch of salt to balance the flavor notes.

Tempering the Chocolate:

To achieve optimal texture and shine, cool the chocolate mass by stirring to about 26-27°C (78.8-80.6°F) and then heat it again to 28-29°C (82.4-84.2°F).

Pouring and Setting:

Pour the chocolate mixture into prepared chocolate molds. Use a spatel to ensure even distribution.
Let the chocolate set at room temperature, which can take 1-2 hours depending on the room climate.

Serving:

Once the chocolate has set, release it from the molds and break or cut it into pieces.

Pear-Gorgonzola Dream is a unique combination of the sweetness of pears and the spicy, cheese-like flavor, nestled in creamy white chocolate. A creation that piques curiosity and invites experimentation.

Pear-Gorgonzola Dream offers an extraordinary taste experience that transcends traditional boundaries and celebrates culinary diversity. Perfect for those who appreciate innovative and daring chocolate creations.

FAQ: Frequently Asked Questions About Vegan Chocolate Making

In this chapter, you will find answers to some of the most common questions newcomers might have in the world of vegan chocolate making. It serves as a practical resource to find quick solutions for common challenges and to deepen your knowledge.

- **What makes chocolate vegan?**
  Vegan chocolate omits all animal products. Instead of dairy, plant-based alternatives such as almond, soy, or coconut milk are used. The main ingredients are cocoa mass, cocoa butter, and plant-based sweeteners.

- **Can I replace regular milk with any plant-based milk?**
  Yes, you can replace animal milk with plant-based alternatives in most recipes. However, consider the taste differences and the consistency of the various plant-based milks.

- **How do I temper chocolate?**
  Tempering is the process of heating and cooling chocolate to achieve a specific crystal structure. This ensures glossiness and snap. Dark chocolate is heated to 45°C, cooled to 28°C, and then reheated to 31-32°C. Similar, slightly adjusted temperatures apply for milk and white chocolate.

- **How long does vegan chocolate last?**
  When properly stored, vegan chocolate can last several months. Storing in a cool, dry place away from strong odors is crucial.

- **Can I replace sugar with other sweeteners?**
  Yes, you can replace sugar with other sweeteners such as maple syrup, agave nectar, or stevia. Note that liquid sweeteners can affect the consistency of the chocolate.

Glossary

To help you get started in vegan chocolate making, here is a glossary of important terms:

Conching: A process where chocolate mass is intensely stirred to refine the texture and reduce unwanted acids and other volatile substances.

Cocoa Butter: The fat extracted from cocoa beans, and a main component of chocolate, responsible for its creamy texture.

Cocoa Mass: The product formed when roasted cocoa beans are ground. It forms the base for making chocolate.

Tempering: A process of heating and cooling chocolate to specific temperatures to achieve a certain crystal form that gives the chocolate gloss and a firm texture.

Vegan Milk Powder: Dried forms of plant milk used as a dairy substitute in making vegan milk chocolate.

With this FAQ and glossary, you now have a solid foundation and a reference tool to assist you in vegan chocolate making.

Closing Words

Dear readers,

We have reached the end of our shared journey through the world of vegan chocolate creations. It has been a voyage of discovery filled with flavors, textures, and unexpected combinations that demonstrate how versatile and inspiring plant-based cuisine can be. Each creation tells its own story, a tribute to nature and its countless gifts.

I hope this book has not only tantalized your taste buds but also touched your heart and filled your kitchens with joy and creativity. Perhaps it has reminded you of familiar flavors or emboldened you to discover new favorites. Maybe it has even inspired you to venture into creating your own.

Your feedback is immensely valuable to me. It is the guide that helps me grow, learn, and evolve. If you have enjoyed this book, I kindly ask you to share your experiences and leave a review. Your words can help others embark on this delicious journey and support me in creating more content that delights your culinary heart.

From the bottom of my heart, I thank you for joining me on this chocolaty adventure. May every day offer you a reason to smile, just as a fine piece of chocolate can.

With sweet regards and in anticipation of your valuable feedback,

Stefan Kronas

Made in the USA
Las Vegas, NV
05 November 2024

11159846R00070